Information liberation

By the same author

The Bias of Science (1979)

Changing the Cogs:
Activists and the Politics of Technology (1979)

Nuclear Knights (1980)

Uprooting War (1984)*

Intellectual Suppression:
Australian Case Histories, Analysis and Responses (co-editor) (1986)

Scientific Knowledge in Controversy:
The Social Dynamics of the Fluoridation Debate (1991)

Strip the Experts (1991)*

Social Defence, Social Change (1993)*

Confronting the Experts (editor) (1996)

Suppression Stories (1997)

* FREEDOM PRESS titles

Information liberation
Challenging the corruptions of information power

Brian Martin

FREEDOM PRESS
London
1998

First published
1998
by Freedom Press
84b Whitechapel High Street
London E1 7QX

ISBN 0 900384 93 X

printed in Great Britain
by Aldgate Press, Gunthorpe Street, London E1 7RQ

Contents

About Freedom Press

Freedom Press was founded in 1886 by a group which included Charlotte Wilson and Peter Kropotkin. Its publication *Freedom*, currrently a fortnightly, is the oldest anarchist newspaper in continuous production.

Other publications include *The Raven*, a quarterly of anarchist thought begun in 1987, and some 70 book titles currently in print. Authors range from anarchist classics like Kropotkin, Malatesta, Rudolf Rocker, Alexander Berkman and Emma Goldman, to contemporary thinkers like Harold Barclay, Colin Ward and Murray Bookchin.

Subjects include anthropology, economics, ecology, education, utopias, capitalism, the state, war and peace, children, land, housing, transport and much more, and the arts are not neglected. There is a set of portrait/biography cards by Clifford Harper, several books of hilarious anarchist strip cartoons, a book of photographs and a children's story book.

Freedom Press is also the wholesale distributor for several other anarchist publishers, and runs a retail bookshop in Angel Alley alongside Whitechapel Art Gallery, open six days a week, selling books on anarchism and related subjects from all sorts of publishers, over the counter and by mail.

Please send for the *Freedom Press Bookshop Catalogue*, and a free specimen copy of *Freedom*.

FREEDOM PRESS (in Angel Alley)
84b Whitechapel High Street,
London E1 7QX

Acknowledgments

Chapter 1: I thank David Mercer for helpful discussions and Mary Cawte for obtaining reference material about Lord Acton.

Chapter 2 is adapted from "Beyond mass media," *Metro Magazine,* No. 101, 1995, pp. 17-23. For helpful comments on drafts, I thank Stan Aungles, Robert Burrowes, Mary Cawte, Edward Herman, Peter McGregor, Will Rifkin, Anna Salleh, Carl Watner and John Zube.

Chapter 3 is adapted from "Against intellectual property," *Philosophy and Social Action,* Vol. 21, No. 3, July-September 1995, pp. 7-22. For helpful discussion, comments and information, I thank Paul Carpenter, Mary Cawte, Peter Drahos, Don Eldridge, Steve Fuller, Keith Graham, Tony Lauck, Dave Ljung, Sandra Mercado, Brian Rappert, Jerry Ravetz, Vernon Richards, Neil Rickert, Dave Roberts, Wendy Varney, David Vaver, Ian Watson, John Zube and anonymous commentators.

Chapter 4 is adapted from "Antisurveillance," *Anarchist Studies,* Vol. 1, No. 2, 1993, pp. 111-129. For helpful discussion and comments on drafts, I thank Stan Aungles, Richard Badham, Sharon Beder, Jim Falk, Oscar Gandy, Jr., Richard Joseph, Dave Keenan, Gary Marx, Jim Rule, Pam Scott and an anonymous referee.

The section in chapter 5 on Bauman's treatment of the Holocaust is adapted from my column in Whistleblowers Australia's newsletter *The Whistle,* January 1997.

Chapter 6 is adapted from the leaflet "Defamation law and free speech," first published by Whistleblowers Australia in September 1996. For extensive advice and comment on drafts, I thank Richard Blake, Sharon Callaghan, Michael Curtis, Don Eldridge, Chris Fox, Judith Gibson, Mary Heath and Mick Skrijel.

The boxed points in chapter 7 are adapted from "What should be done about higher education?" *Social Anarchism,* No. 14, 1989, pp. 30-39. Blanca Facundo made useful comments on chapter 9.

For helpful comments on the entire manuscript, I thank Lyn Carson, Richard Gosden, Wendy Varney and Danny Yee.

I would be happy to correspond with anyone concerning the matters covered in this book. Contact me at brian_martin@uow.edu.au or Science and Technology Studies, University of Wollongong, NSW 2522, Australia.

1

Power tends to corrupt

Power tends to corrupt, and absolute power corrupts absolutely.
This familiar saying originated as a comment in a letter written
by Lord Acton, an English historian who lived from 1834 to
1902. His full name was John Emerich Edward Dahlberg Acton.
He was a fierce opponent of state power, whether the state was
democratic, socialist or authoritarian.

Acton's aphorism has outlasted his other contributions
because it captures an insight that rings true to many people.
Power certainly seems to corrupt quite a few politicians. Early in
their careers, many of them are eager to change the system. They
want to help the poor and disadvantaged and to root out corruption and unjust privilege. Yet when they actually get into
positions of power, it's a different story. The old slogans become
memories. Instead, it becomes a higher priority to placate and
reward powerful bureaucracies in both the government and
corporate sectors. Most of all, it becomes a priority to increase
the power and wealth of politicians themselves.

In the 1960s the so-called "new left" demanded power to the
people. But how to achieve it? Some activists advocated the
"long march through institutions"—in other words, left-wingers
should work through the system to get into positions of power,
climbing the ladder in government bureaucracies, corporations,
political parties, professions and universities. *Then* they would
be able to bring about desirable social change. Unfortunately,
this strategy doesn't work. The institutions change the activists
long before the activists have a chance to change the institutions.

The idea that power tends to corrupt has an intuitive appeal, but is there anything more to it? A few social scientists have studied the corrupting effects of power.

Pioneering sociologist Robert Michels studied the tendency of political parties to become less democratic. Even in the most revolutionary parties, the leaders have gained greater power and become entrenched in their positions. The party organisation becomes an end in itself, more important than the party's original aim. Michels concluded that every organisation is affected by these tendencies.[1]

Pitirim Sorokin and Walter Lunden examined the behaviour of powerful leaders, such as kings of England. They found that those with the greatest power were far more likely to commit crimes, such as theft and murder, than ordinary citizens.[2] This is striking evidence that power tends to corrupt.

But why does power corrupt? For the answer, it is worth consulting the excellent work by David Kipnis, a psychology researcher at Temple University.

For a person to be autonomous is widely considered to be a good thing. It is a feature of being fully human. When a person exercises power over others, the powerholder gains the impression that the others do not control their own behaviour or, in other words, they are not autonomous. Hence, they are seen as less worthy. In short, a person who successfully exercises power over others is more likely to believe that these others are less deserving of respect. They thus become good prospects to be exploited.

Kipnis organised numerous experiments to explore such dynamics. In one experiment, a "boss" oversaw the work of

---

[1] Robert Michels, *Political Parties: A Sociological Study of the Oligarchical Tendencies of Modern Democracies,* translated by Eden & Cedar Paul (New York: Dover, 1959; Hearst's International Library, 1915).

[2] Pitirim A. Sorokin and Walter A. Lunden, *Power and Morality: Who Shall Guard the Guardians?* (Boston: Porter Sargent, 1959). See also David R. Simon and D. Stanley Eitzen, *Elite Deviance* (Boston: Allyn & Bacon, 1982).

"subordinates" in a simulated situation. The experiment was contrived so that all subordinates did exactly the same work. But the subordinate who was thought to be self-motivated was rated to have done better work than the subordinate who was thought to have done the work only under instruction. As well as laboratory studies, Kipnis examined the effects of power on the powerholder through studies of couples, managers and protagonists in Shakespeare's dramas. The results were always the same.

Kipnis followed through the implications of such evidence in a number of areas involving technology, including medical technology, workplace technology and the technology of repression. For example, technologies for surveillance or torture serve to control others: that is the obvious effect. But in addition, the psychology of the powerholder is changed when the technology promotes the reality or impression that others lack autonomy. Those subject to the technology are treated as less worthy, and any prospects for equality are undermined.

Kipnis also deals with tactics of influence, use of rewards, inhibition of the exercise of power, motivations for power and other corruptions of power. This work is extremely valuable for better understanding the psychological dynamics of power.[3]

If power tends to corrupt, what are the implications? One response is to try to impose controls on powerholders: codes of ethics, agreements, laws. For example, having nuclear weapons gives governments a lot of power. So international agreements are made to control these weapons, such as hot lines to communicate in a crisis, treaties on numbers of weapons and promises to not launch a first strike. But this doesn't get to the heart of the problem. As long as nuclear weapons exist, a great amount of power rests in the hands of those few individuals who control them. This is corrupting and the danger of nuclear war persists.

---

[3] David Kipnis, *The Powerholders* (Chicago: University of Chicago Press, 1981, 2nd edition); David Kipnis, *Technology and Power* (New York: Springer-Verlag, 1990).

The alternative is to abolish nuclear weapons so that inequalities inherent in the power of nuclear weaponry do not exist. More generally, the corruptions of power can be minimised by equalising power and opposing social and technological systems that foster power inequalities. This works out the same as opposing systems of domination, inequality and exploitation. In this picture, a free society is a society with the least power differences. This does not mean a stable society of identical citizens. Instead, it could easily be a society seething with action and conflict, precisely because everyone has opportunities to exercise significant power. The point is that there would be no social structures or technologies—such as bureaucracies and nuclear weapons—that give some individuals a great deal of power over others.

The idea of a free society should be seen as a method, not an end point. The idea that "power tends to corrupt" is a guide to action. Policies, technologies and organisational arrangements can be judged to see whether they contribute to equality or inequality of power.

This can easily be applied to information. Information is a part of all systems of power. Top bureaucrats try to control information as part of their control over subordinates and clients. Corporations try to control information through trade secrets and patents. Militaries try to control information using the rationale of "national security." So-called freedom of information—namely, public access to documents produced in bureaucracies—is a threat to top bureaucrats.

In a society where not everyone can read and write, literacy is a form of power and campaigns for mass literacy are a threat to ruling elites. In a society where employees cannot speak freely due to fears about job security, bosses hold power and campaigns for workers' control are a threat to top managers. In a society where a few owners and editors control systems of mass communication, campaigns for multiple independent avenues for publication are a threat to elites.

This book applies Acton's insight about the corruptions of power to various areas dealing with information and communication. I don't cover every topic but try to illustrate some ways to proceed.

- The mass media are inherently undemocratic because a small number of individuals control what is communicated to a large audience (chapter 2).
- Patents and copyrights give control over use of information to corporations and individuals. This power is commonly used to benefit the rich and exploit the poor (chapter 3).
- Surveillance, which boils down to gathering information about someone else without their knowledge or consent, is a method for social control (chapter 4).
- Employees do not have free speech (chapter 5).
- Defamation law is regularly used to suppress free speech (chapter 6).
- The structure of research organisations, including universities, makes knowledge mainly useful to governments, corporations, professions and researchers themselves (chapter 7).
- Ideas that will be useful for popular understanding and action need to be simple in essence—though not just any simple idea will serve the purpose (chapter 8).
- People need to learn to think for themselves rather than accept the ideas of famous intellectuals (chapter 9).

Information plays a role in nearly every field of human activity, from art to industry, and all of these are subject to the corruptions of power. Challenging information-related systems of power is one avenue for social change. But it's only one of many possible avenues. Bringing about a just society involves more than achieving a goal involving knowledge and communication, such as equal access to information. Also needed are changes in personal relations, economics, military systems and many other areas. Challenging the corruptions of information power is just one way to proceed—but it is an important and fascinating one.

Some rough definitions

- *Information* is data that has been processed, organised or classified into categories.

- *Knowledge* is facts and principles believed to be true.

- *Wisdom* is good judgement of what is useful for achieving something worthwhile.

Information without knowledge isn't much use, and knowledge without wisdom isn't much use. More information isn't necessarily a good thing without the capacity to interpret, understand and use it. Nevertheless, the focus here is on power to control information, which has consequences for developing knowledge and wisdom.

2

Beyond mass media

Mass media are inherently corrupting. A small number of owners and editors exercise great power over what is communicated to large numbers of people. Mass media should be replaced by participatory media organised as networks, such as telephone and computer networks. Strategies to supersede mass media include changing one's own media consumption patterns, participating in alternative media and using nonviolent action against the mass media.

Complaints about the mass media are commonplace. To begin, there is the low quality of many of the programmes and articles. There is the regular portrayal of violence, given an attention out of proportion with its frequency in everyday life. More generally, most of the mass media give much more attention to crime, deaths, disasters, wars and strife than to harmonious communities, acts of kindness and win-win conflict resolution. The mass media frequently create unrealistic fears about criminals, foreign peoples and mass protest.

"News" often is more like entertainment than information or education. News reports, especially on television, are typically given without much overt context. The latest events are described, but there is no explanation of what led up to them or caused them. Consumers of the media consequently hear a lot of facts but frequently don't understand how they fit together. "Context" is the result of the assumptions behind the facts, and

7

this context is all the more powerful because it is neither stated nor discussed.

Even the "facts" that are presented are often wrong or misleading. Powerful groups, especially governments and large corporations, shape the news in a range of ways, such as by providing selected information, offering access to stories in exchange for favourable coverage, spreading disinformation, and threatening reprisals.

Advertising is another powerful influence on commercial media. Advertisers influence what types of stories are presented. But more deeply, advertisements themselves shape people's views of the world. They are a pervasive source of unreality, fostering insecurity and consumerism.

There are indeed many problems with the mass media. But some media are much better than others, judged by the criteria of accuracy, quality and independence of special interests. Most media critics seem to believe that it is possible to promote and develop enlightened, responsive, truly educative mass media. Efforts at reform can be worthwhile, but have intrinsic limits.

The problem is not with media in general, but with *mass* media, namely those media that are produced by relatively few people compared to the number who receive them. Most large newspapers, television and radio stations fit this description. Mass media by their nature give power to a few and offer little scope for participation by the vast majority. The power of the mass media is corrupting. The only surprise is how responsible some mass media are. Given the corruptions of power, reform of the mass media, although useful, should not be the goal. Instead, the aim should be to replace mass media by communication systems that are more participatory.

The usual approaches

Most analyses of the media assume that there are just two choices, either state control or a free market. The problem with control by the state is that control is centralised. The media of military regimes and bureaucratic socialist states are notorious for their censorship. The defenders of the "free market" argue that government-owned media, or tight regulations, are similarly noxious even in liberal democracies.

The problem with "free market" media is that they give only a very limited freedom, namely freedom for large media companies and other powerful corporate interests.[1] Everyone is "free" to own a publishing company or television station.

The limitations of the mass media in liberal democracies are not always easy to perceive unless one has access to alternative sources of information. Fortunately, there are some excellent books and magazines that expose the incredible biases, cover-ups and misleading perspectives in the mass media. The magazines *Extra!, Free Press, Lies of our Times* and *Reportage* give eye-opening accounts of the ways in which the English-language mass media give flattering perspectives of business and government, limit coverage of issues affecting women and minorities, cover up elite corruption, promote government policy agendas, and so forth. The book *Unreliable Sources* gives examples of the conservative, establishment and corporate bias of US mass media on issues such as politicians, foreign affairs, environment, racism, terrorism and human rights.[2] Intriguingly, conservatives also believe that the media are biased, but against *them*.[3]

The analysis that underlies these exposés is simple and effective: corporations and governments have a large influence on the mass media, and the mass media *are* big businesses themselves. These factors appear to explain most of the problems. The power of the western mass media is especially damaging to the interests

---

[1] Lichtenberg, Judith. 1987. "Foundations and limits of freedom of the press," *Philosophy and Public Affairs*, Vol. 16, No. 4, Fall, pp. 329-355.

[2] Martin A. Lee and Norman Solomon, *Unreliable Sources: A Guide to Detecting Bias in News Media* (New York: Carol, 1990).

[3] George Comstock, *Television in America* (Beverly Hills: Sage, 1980), pp. 50-56, reports that about equal numbers of viewers believe that US television is biased towards either liberal or conservative viewpoints.

of Third World peoples, being an integral part of contemporary cultural imperialism.[4]

Yes, the media are biased. What can be done about it? Jeff Cohen, of Fairness and Accuracy in Reporting (FAIR), has a strategy. He says

- be sceptical of media stories;
- write letters to media companies, make complaints, join talk-back radio;
- don't advocate censorship, but instead advocate presentation of both sides on any issue;
- use public access TV;
- hold meetings and pickets;
- use alternative media.[5]

This is a good grassroots approach. But the goal is "fairness and accuracy," namely the balancing of news. There seems to be no larger programme to replace undemocratic media structures.

A sophisticated treatment of these issues is given by John

---

[4] See especially the now classic treatment by Ben Bagdikian, *The Media Monopoly* (Boston: Beacon Press, 1993, 4th edition). Two hard-hitting attacks on corporate domination of information and culture, focussing on the US, are Herbert I. Schiller, *Culture, Inc.: The Corporate Takeover of Public Expression* (New York: Oxford University Press, 1989) and Gerald Sussman, *Communication, Technology, and Politics in the Information Age* (Thousand Oaks, CA: Sage, 1997). In terms of how the dominant influences on the media operate, one can choose between a propaganda model as given by Edward S. Herman and Noam Chomsky, *Manufacturing Consent: The Political Economy of the Mass Media* (New York: Pantheon, 1988)—based on the five filters of ownership, advertising, sourcing from powerful organisations, attacks on unwelcome programmes, and anticommunism—or a model involving organisational imperatives and journalistic practices as given by W. Lance Bennett, *News: The Politics of Illusion* (New York: Longman, 1988, 2nd edition) and Rodney Tiffen, *News and Power* (Sydney: Allen and Unwin, 1989), among others. For the purposes here, the differences between these analyses are not important. For many other sources, see James R. Bennett, *Control of the Media in the United States: An Annotated Bibliography* (Hamden, CT: Garland, 1992).

[5] Lee and Solomon (see note 2), pp. 340-358.

Keane in his book *The Media and Democracy*.[6] He provides an elegant critique of "market liberalism," the approach by which governments reduce their intervention in communication markets. He notes that unregulated communication markets actually restrict communication freedom by creating monopolies, setting up barriers to entry and turning knowledge into a commodity. He also points out several trends in liberal democracies that seem to be of no concern to supporters of a free market in communication: the use of government emergency powers, secret operations by the military and police, lying by politicians, advertising by governments, and increasing collaboration between elites in government, business and trade unions. The increasingly global reach of communication corporations is also a significant problem.

The traditional alternative to commercial media is "public service media," namely government-financed media (such as the ABC in Australia, BBC in Britain and CBC in Canada) combined with government regulation of commercial media. Keane favours revived public service media, with guaranteed autonomy of government-funded media, government regulation of commercial media, and support for non-state, non-market media, a category that includes small presses and magazines, community radio stations and open-access television stations.

Keane's model sounds very good in theory. He gives an imposing list of things that *should* be done, but he doesn't say *who* is going to make it happen—the government, presumably. More deeply, Keane doesn't say how the state itself will be controlled. He wants a new constitutional settlement with enlightened and progressive government media, suitable government controls on commercial media, and promotion of the "non-state, non-market media." But why should "the state" do all this? Why won't it keep doing what it is already doing, as he describes so well?

---

6 John Keane, *The Media and Democracy* (London: Polity Press, 1991).

Limits to participation

In principle, the mass media could be quite democratic, if only they were run differently. Editorial independence could be guaranteed, minimising the influence of government, owners or other special interest groups. A range of viewpoints could be presented. The power of advertisers could be reduced or eliminated. Opportunities for citizen input into content could be opened up. These are worthy goals. But there are inherent limits to making mass media truly democratic.

Consider, for example, an alternative newspaper with a substantial circulation and reputation. The editors may be highly responsive to readers, but even so some editorial decisions must be made. Choices must be made about what stories to run, which advertisements to accept (if any), which events to publicise, which submissions to accept, what policies to make about language, and so forth. There are innumerable "policy" decisions to be made. Even spelling can be controversial. Should the paper be open to the debate about spelling reform? What about letters to the editor? Should everything be published, or should some selection be made on the basis of topic or quality?

If there are only a few active contributors, then everyone can be involved who wants to be, and all submissions published. But this is extremely unlikely when the circulation becomes large and the publication is seen to be important. Then lots of people see an opportunity to raise their own favourite issues.

These problems are far from hypothetical. They are quite apparent to anyone dealing with alternative magazines with circulations in the tens of thousands, or even just thousands. Not everyone who wants to can have an article published in *Mother Jones, New Statesman and Society* or *The Progressive.* Such magazines are "high quality" because they are able to select from many potential offerings. But being able to select also means that the editors have a great deal of power. Being able to define and select "quality" also means being able to make decisions about content.

Of course, from the point of view of the owners and editors of such magazines, they are hard pressed just to survive. Make some wrong decisions and readership may drop off or financial benefactors may be less generous. (Most "alternative" magazines depend heavily on contributions to supplement subscription fees.) Practising "democracy" within such a magazine, if this means publishing letters from all and sundry or letting readers vote on policy matters, would be a prescription for financial disaster.

These comments are a bit unfair to the alternative media. By definition, even the largest of them is still a small player in the media game. Furthermore, a diversity of perspectives is available through the different alternative media. There are more small magazines available than anyone can read. My point is not to criticise the alternative media, but to point out that participatory democracy is virtually impossible in a medium where a small number of owners and editors produce a product for a much larger audience.

The futility of seeking media democracy becomes even more apparent when the scale is increased: audiences of hundreds of thousands or millions. This is the domain of major newspapers, television stations and wire services. It requires only a little analysis to find that the larger the audience, the more powerful are the key decision-makers in the media organisations and the less effective are any mechanisms for participation. The very scale of the media limits opportunities for participation and increases the power of key figures. The way in which this power is used depends on the relation of the media to the most powerful groups in society. In liberal democracies, governments and corporations, and media corporations in particular, exercise the greatest power over the media. The large scale of the mass media is what makes it possible for this power to be exercised so effectively.

Other arguments for mass media?

Before dismissing mass media, it is worth seeing whether there are other justifications for them. Perhaps there are some overlooked arguments for maintaining mass media even in a fully participatory society. It is worth canvassing a few of them.

Emergencies

The mass media, especially radio and television, can come in handy in emergencies: messages can be broadcast, reaching a large fraction of the population.

But the mass media are not really necessary for emergency purposes. Fire alarms, for example, do not rely on conventional media. Furthermore, network media, including telephone and computer networks, can be set up to allow emergency communications.

Actually, the mass media are a great vulnerability in certain emergencies: military coups. Because they allow a few people to communicate to a large population with little possibility of dialogue, television and radio stations are commonly the first targets in military takeovers. Censorship of newspapers is a next step. This connection between coups and mass media also highlights the role of mass media in authoritarian regimes.

Military strength is no defence against a military coup, and indeed may be the cause of one. To resist a coup, network communications are far superior to mass media.[7] So, from the point of view of preparing for emergencies, mass media are bad investments.

Media talent

The mass media allow many people to enjoy and learn from the efforts of some highly talented performers and personalities, including actors, musicians, athletes, journalists and commentators. True. But even without mass media, it is possible for people

---

[7] Brian Martin, "Communication technology and nonviolent action," *Media Development,* Vol. 43, No. 2, 1996, pp. 3-9.

to enjoy and learn from these talented individuals, for example through audio and video recordings.

Furthermore, the mass media limit access to all but a few performers and contributors. Those who are left out have a much better chance of reaching a sympathetic audience via network media.

A force for good

The mass media are undoubtedly powerful. In the right hands, they can be a powerful force for good purposes. Therefore, it might be argued, the aim should be to promote a mass media that is overseen by responsible, accountable people.

This sounds like a good argument. What it overlooks is how easily power corrupts. Whoever has power in the mass media is susceptible to the corruptions of power, including power sought for its own sake and for self-enrichment.

Large resources

The mass media command enormous resources, both financial and symbolic. This makes it possible for them to pursue large or expensive projects such as large-budget films, special investigative teams and in-depth coverage of key events.

Actually, large-scale projects are also possible with network systems. They simply require cooperation and collaboration. For example, some public domain software (free computer programs) is quite sophisticated and has been produced with the help of many people. In centralised systems, far-reaching decisions can be made by just a few people. In decentralised systems, greater participation is required.

* * *

These four possible arguments for retaining mass media, in some reformed and improved form, actually turn out to be arguments against mass media. The mass media are not necessary for emergencies and are actually a key vulnerability to those who would take over a society. The mass media are not necessary to enjoy and benefit from the talent of others. Power exercised through the mass media is unlikely to be a force for good since it tends to corrupt those who exercise it. Finally, although the mass media can undertake large projects, such projects can also develop through network media, but in a way involving participation rather than central direction.

Participatory media

In order to better understand the mass media's inherent lack of democracy, it is useful to imagine a communication system that allows and fosters participation by everyone. David Andrews did this with his concept of "information routeing groups" or IRGs.[8] His discussion predated the vast expansion of computer networks and is worth outlining in its original form. He imagined a computer network in which everyone is linked to several interest groups, with each group having anywhere from perhaps half a dozen up to several hundred people. An interest group might deal with anything from growing apples to racism. Each time a person makes a contribution on a topic, whether a short comment, a picture or a substantial piece of writing, they send it to everyone in the group. A person receiving a message could, if they wished, post it to other groups to which they belonged. Andrews called each of the groups an IRG.

In a network of IRGs, everyone can be a writer and publisher at the same time. But there are no guaranteed mass audiences. If a contribution is really important or exciting to those who receive it, they are more likely to post it to other groups. In this way, a piece of writing could end up being read by thousands or even millions of people. But note that this requires numerous individual decisions about circulating it to further groups. In the case of the mass media, a single editor can make the decision to run or stop an item. In the case of IRGs, lots of people are involved. By deciding whether or not to forward an item to another group, each person acts somewhat like an editor.

---

[8] David Andrews, *The IRG Solution: Hierarchical Incompetence and How to Overcome It* (London: Souvenir Press, 1984).

A system of IRGs can be self-limiting. If a group has too many active members, then each one might be bombarded with hundreds of messages every day. Some might opt out, as long as there was someone who would select pertinent messages for them. This person then acts as a type of editor. But note that this "editor" has little of the formal power of editors in the mass media. In an IRG system, anyone can set themselves up as an editor of this sort. Members of this editor's IRG can easily look at the larger body of contributions, should they so wish. One of the main reasons why the IRG editor has relatively little formal power is that there is no substantial investment in terms of subscriptions, advertisers, printing equipment or salaries. Participating in an IRG is something that can easily be done in a few hours per week. Investments are lower and positions are less entrenched. An IRG editor will maintain an audience only as long as the editing is perceived to be effective. Similarly, quitting is relatively painless.

To anyone familiar with computer networks, especially the Internet, it may seem that to talk about IRGs is simply an awkward way of describing what is actually taking place on existing networks. Indeed, Andrews' account of IRGs can be interpreted as a description of what later took place on the Internet. While parts of the Internet operate like IRGs, it is unwise to assume that cyberspace is or will remain a model participatory medium. There are ongoing pressures, inequalities and struggles involving access, cost, commercial uses, censorship and surveillance.

IRGs do not have to be based on computers. They can operate—though more slowly—using the postal system. Again, this already happens with a number of discussions that operate by post, where each member adds a page or so of comment on the current topic and sends it to the group coordinator, who then makes copies of all contributions for all members. For those who have the technology and know how to use it, computer networks make this process far easier and faster.

Another medium that is inherently participatory is the telephone. Phones are very easy to use—only speaking, not writing, is required—and are widely available. Certainly it is possible for a person to dominate a telephone conversation, but only one person is at the other end of the line, or occasionally more in the case of a conference call. In the mass media, one person speaks and thousands or millions hear.

Ivan Illich proposed the concept of "convivial tools."[9] This includes technologies that foster creative and autonomous interactions between people. Convivial technologies in the case of the media are the ones that foster participation. The postal system, the telephone system, computer networks and short-wave radio are examples of convivial media.

The implication of this analysis is straightforward. To promote a more participatory society, it is important to promote participatory media and to challenge, replace and eventually abandon mass media. Jerry Mander, in his case against television, gave as one of his four main arguments corporate domination of television used to mould humans for a commercial environment.[10] But all mass media involve centralised power. Mander's argument should be extended: all mass media should be abandoned.

Saying "mass media should be superseded" is easy. Working out practical implications is the hard part. In my view, although a world without mass media may be a long-term goal, the mass media will be around for quite some time. Therefore, it is necessary to have a strategy to challenge them, from inside and outside, as well as to promote alternatives.

There are already plenty of challenges to the mass media, of course. But these challenges are not to the existence of the mass media, but only to the way they are run. In a way, media criticism is a form of loyal opposition.

---

9   Ivan Illich, *Tools for Conviviality* (London: Calder and Boyars, 1973).
10 Jerry Mander, *Four Arguments for the Elimination of Television* (New York: William Morrow, 1978).

Wait—before looking at strategies, what if the mass media are being whittled away anyway? Are cable television and the Internet making mass media obsolete by providing more communication channels and creating niche markets? Will newspapers be replaced by net-based news services that can be individually tailored? Is the mass audience a relic of the modernist age, while fragmentation of audiences and perspectives is characteristic of the new postmodern era?

It would be unwise to trust in "natural" processes to cause the demise of mass media. There is nothing automatic about technological and social change. Powerful groups are doing everything they can to control markets and opinions in the changing information order. Another scenario is that mass media will continue to have a major influence and that governments and corporations will extend their influence into the more fragmented channels. After all, television, video cameras and cassettes did not lead to the collapse of Hollywood and large-scale movie-making. If the mass media are ever replaced, it will be due to lots of people taking action to help it happen. Hence the need for strategies, both individual and collective.

Strategies

Here I outline a number of possible strategies, focussing on what can be done by individuals and small groups to challenge mass media and replace them by participatory network media. It would be easy to make some sweeping recommendations about what *should* be done, especially by governments. But to be compatible with the goal of a participatory communication system, the methods should be participatory too. The following ideas are meant to encourage discussion.

Change one's own media consumption patterns

Many people are such regular and insistent consumers of the mass media—television, radio and newspapers—that it's possible to speak of an addiction. This also includes many of those who are strongly critical of the mass media. Cutting down on consumption can be part of a process of imagining and fostering a participatory communications system.

Some people may object to this recommendation. Surely, they will say, it's quite possible to be an avid mass media consumer— or to work for the media—while still maintaining a critical perspective and also using and promoting alternative media. True enough. Analogously, a factory worker can certainly remain critical of capitalism and promote alternatives.

My view is not that cutting back mass media consumption is necessary, but that it can be a useful way to change people's consciousness. It is similar to animal liberationists reducing their consumption of animal products and environmentalists riding bicycles and composting their organic wastes. Such individual acts cannot by themselves transform the underlying structures of factory farming, industrial society or centralised media: collective action for structural change is needed. Nevertheless, changes in individual behaviour serve several important purposes: they change the perspectives of individuals, they reinforce concern about the issue and they provide an example (of consistency) for others.

Changing media habits can be incredibly difficult. Watching the news on television is, for many people, a ritual. For others, reading the daily paper is an essential part of each day. Although Jerry Mander's book *Four Arguments for the Elimination of Television* has become a classic in alternative circles, no social movement has developed to abolish TV. There are only some small groups, such as the Society for the Elimination of Television, producing a few newsletters.

One reason may be that—according to one argument— watching television changes one's brain waves, reducing the number of fast waves characteristic of thinking and increasing the number of slow waves characteristic of relaxed states. This explains why watching television seems so relaxing: it allows the brain to switch off. It also explains why television is so effective at communicating commercial messages. Images go into the brain without processing; the images cannot be recalled, but they can be recognised, for example in a supermarket.[11]

Another reason why switching off the television is so difficult is that it becomes part of the household. It *seems* voluntary, and it is to some extent. Action must begin at home.[12] It is easier to oppose "alien" technologies such as nuclear power, which are not part of people's everyday lives. Challenging technologies that are personal possessions, used routinely—such as television and cars—is far more difficult.

Except for some people who must monitor the media as part of their work, mass media consumption is, from a time management view, quite inefficient. Think back on all the television you watched during the past ten years. How much of it was genuinely necessary to be fully informed, or was even genuinely informative? A similar calculation can be made for reading newspapers.

But what if the aim is not efficiency but simply enjoying life and occasionally learning something along the way? This brings the discussion back to lack of participation. Most people have been turned into passive consumers of the media. This will not change until some people take the initiative to break the pattern.

Learn how the media construct reality

If it is essential to consume products of the mass media, a useful antidote is to learn how these media products are created. It is illuminating to spend time with a television film crew or in a newspaper office. It quickly becomes apparent that of the many possible things that could be treated by the media, and of the many possible ways that this could be done, only certain ones actually are chosen. It is also useful to gain some experience on

---

[11] Fred Emery and Merrelyn Emery, *A Choice of Futures: To Enlighten or Inform* (Leiden: Martinus Nijhoff, 1976).

[12] Frances Moore Lappé and Family, *What to Do After You Turn Off the TV: Fresh Ideas for Enjoying Family Life* (New York: Ballantine Books, 1985); Martin Large, *Who's Bringing Them Up? Television and Child Development* (Gloucester: Martin Large, 1980).

the receiving end of media construction of reality, by joining a rally or media conference and seeing how it is reported, or by being interviewed oneself.

Another way to gain insight into media construction of reality is to undertake a detailed study of some topic, whether it is child rearing, banking, crime or East African politics. This could involve reading books and in-depth articles, investigating alternative viewpoints and consulting with experts and concerned groups. With a good grounding in a range of perspectives and an ability to think confidently about the topic, it is then possible to make an informed assessment of mass media treatments, including biases and omissions.

It is important to be aware of how the media constructs reality, but that alone does not change the dynamics of the media. Therefore it is valuable to communicate what one learns about media constructions to others.

Participate in a group to change media consumption patterns

In a group of two or more people, it can be easier to make some of the individual changes. Individuals can be assigned the task of monitoring particular media and reporting on issues that are important to the group. Others can do the same with alternative media. In this way, individuals don't need to worry so much that they have missed some important item. More important, though, is the process of interaction in the group: discussing the issues. This is what is missing in the individual consumption of the mass media.

Of course, quite a bit of discussion occurs already among friends and colleagues. By working in a more directed fashion in a group, a greater commitment to participation and participatory media can be fostered. Teachers can contribute to this process by giving guidance on how to analyse the mass media and how to use and develop alternatives.

Use the mass media for one's own purposes

This is the usual approach: writing letters to the editor, putting out press releases, being interviewed, inviting media to meetings, holding rallies to attract media coverage, etc. Numerous action groups, from feminists to farmers, promote their cause this way.

Such efforts can shift the emphasis in media coverage, for example from coverage of politicians and business to some attention to social issues and movements. But this does little or nothing to challenge the fundamental lack of participation in the mass media. Furthermore, it can distort social movement agendas. Seeking media attention can be a way of building grassroots support but it can also take priority over building support. Some movement leaders are turned into stars by the media, causing internal stresses and resentments.[13] All in all, this approach, as a means of promoting participatory media, has little to recommend it. Social movements need a strategy on communication, including how to deal with both establishment and alternative media.[14]

Of course, promoting participatory media is not the only goal of social movements. In a great number of cases, using the existing mass media is a sensible and quite justifiable approach. Furthermore, campaigns such as those by Fairness and Accuracy in Reporting to challenge biases in the media are extremely important. But it is important to be aware of the limitations of such campaigns. Even "fair and accurate" mass media are far from participatory.

Participating in the mass media is inevitably limited to only a few people or only to minor contributions. Only a few people have the skills or opportunity to write an article—that will be

---

[13] Todd Gitlin, *The Whole World is Watching: Mass Media in the Making and Unmaking of the New Left* (Berkeley: University of California Press, 1980).

[14] Marc Raboy, *Movements and Messages: Media and Radical Politics in Quebec* (Toronto: Between the Lines, 1984).

published—for a large newspaper, or to be interviewed for more than a few seconds on television. Even an occasional article or television appearance is trivial compared to the impact of those who host a television programme or write a regular column in a major paper. Furthermore, those who are successful in "breaking in" may actually legitimise the media in which they appear. This is analogous to the way that worker representatives on company boards can legitimise both the decisions made and the hierarchical structure of the company.

Many progressives want to use the media, or go into it as journalists or producers, to help the causes in which they believe. The intention is good, and the work many of them do is superb. But it should be remembered that this approach perpetuates unequal participation. It needs to be asked whether the aim is mainly to promote a favoured viewpoint or to foster a discussion involving ever more people. These two aims are not always compatible.

Participate in alternative media

This is an obvious strategy. Possibilities include:

- subscribing to alternative magazines and supporting small .presses;
- writing material for newsletters and small magazines;
- publishing one's own newsletter, magazine or books;
- organising meetings of friends to discuss issues of significance;
- doing community organising with techniques such as public meetings and door-to-door canvassing;
- listening to and producing programmes for community radio and television;
- participating in computer discussion groups;
- producing, collecting and using micrographics (microfiche, microfilm), especially to distribute and save nonstandard works;
- using short-wave radio;

- running workshops on developing skills for network media;
- developing campaigns that help build skills in using alternative media and don't rely on mass media;
- participating in self-managing media enterprises.[15]

These and other initiatives are going on all the time. They need more support and development. This strategy is fully compatible with the goal of participatory media, so there are fewer internal contradictions and traps.

Use nonviolent action to challenge the mass media

Activists have more often used than challenged the mass media. Yet there are numerous methods of nonviolent action that can be used to confront and change mass media, as well as to promote network media.[16] For example, boycotts can be organised of particularly offensive publications or shows. Small shareholders can use direct action to present their concerns at shareholders' meetings. Activists can occupy media offices. However, it is usually extremely difficult for consumers of the media to organise challenges. The best prospects are for media workers. They can challenge and subvert management by publishing or showing items without permission, allowing humorous mistakes to slip through, resigning as a group, working in against orders, and even taking over media operations and running them participatively. Such initiatives can only succeed if there is considerable support from the users of the media. Hence, links between

---

[15] John Downing, *Radical Media: The Political Experience of Alternative Communication* (Boston: South End Press, 1984); Edward Herman, "Democratic media," *Z Papers,* Vol. 1, No. 1, January-March 1992, pp. 23-30. For further references see James R. Bennett (see note 4).

[16] On nonviolent action, see Virginia Coover, Ellen Deacon, Charles Esser and Christopher Moore, *Resource Manual for a Living Revolution* (Philadelphia: New Society Publishers, 1981); Per Herngren, *Path of Resistance: The Practice of Civil Disobedience* (Philadelphia: New Society Publishers, 1993); George Lakey, *Powerful Peacemaking: A Strategy for a Living Revolution* (Philadelphia: New Society Publishers, 1987); Gene Sharp, *The Politics of Nonviolent Action* (Boston: Porter Sargent, 1973).

workers and users are essential, for example between journalists and public interest groups.

Undermine institutional supports for mass media

This is a big one. It roughly translates into "undermine monopoly capitalism and the state."

The mass media would not be able to maintain their dominant position without special protection. Television is the best example. In most countries, governments own and run all channels. In liberal democracies there are some commercial channels, but these must be licensed by the government. Without government regulation, anyone could set up a studio and broadcast at whatever frequency they wanted. For cable systems, government regulations control who gains access.

The power of commercial television comes, of course, from corporate sponsorship, typically via advertisements. Without sponsorship from wealthy corporations, a few channels would be unlikely to be able to maintain their dominant positions. If a society of small enterprises is imagined—whether run by owners or worker collectives—there would be no basis or reason for large-scale sponsorship of mass media.

Corporations and governments also are crucial in maintaining the position of large-circulation newspapers. In many countries the dominant newspapers are government owned and produced. In capitalist societies, advertisements are essential to keep the purchase price down. Without advertisements, the size of the papers would shrink and the price would jump, leading to a decline in circulation. This would make the newspapers more similar to current-day alternative newspapers and magazines, which typically require contributions above and beyond subscription fees in order to stay afloat. Governments also help maintain large-circulation commercial newspapers in various indirect ways, including high postal rates for alternative media, defamation law (which can bankrupt small publishers—see chapter 6), and copyright (which enables monopoly profits—see chapter 3).

Governments and large corporations support the mass media, and vice versa. Of course, there are many conflicts between these powerful groups, such as when the media criticise particular government decisions or corporate actions, and when government or corporations try to muzzle or manipulate the media. But at a more fundamental level, these institutions reinforce each other. Without government and corporate support, the mass media would disintegrate. With participatory media instead of mass media, governments and corporations would be far less able to control information and maintain their legitimacy.

In terms of strategy, the implication of this analysis is that challenges to the mass media, and the strengthening of network media, should be linked to challenges to monopoly capitalism and the state. To bring about participatory media, it is also necessary to bring about participatory alternatives to present economic and political structures.

Conclusion

In order for any significant shift away from the mass media to occur, there must be a dramatic shift in attitudes and behaviours. People who neither watch television nor read newspapers are now commonly seen as eccentrics. A shift needs to occur so that they are supported, and it is the heavy consumers of the mass media who are given little reinforcement. Such shifts are possible. For example, anti-smoking activism has dramatically changed attitudes and policies in a few countries about smoking in public.

In order for withdrawal from using the mass media to become more popular, participatory media must become more attractive: cheaper, more accessible, more fun, more relevant. In such an atmosphere, nonviolent action campaigns against the mass media and in support of participatory media become more feasible. Such campaigns, especially if supported by social movements, in turn make changes in personal media habits more likely and acceptable.

This, in outline, is one way that the mass media might be undermined. But it will not be an easy or quick operation. In so far as modern society is ever more based on information and knowledge, the mass media are increasingly central to the maintenance of unequal power and wealth. This is all the more reason to give special attention to the task of achieving a society without mass media.

3

Against intellectual property

There is a strong case for opposing intellectual property. Among other things, it often retards innovation and exploits Third World peoples. Most of the usual arguments for intellectual property do not hold up under scrutiny. In particular, the metaphor of the marketplace of ideas provides no justification for ownership of ideas. The alternative to intellectual property is that intellectual products not be owned, as in the case of everyday language. Strategies against intellectual property include civil disobedience, promotion of non-owned information, and fostering of a more cooperative society.

The original rationale for copyrights and patents was to foster artistic and practical creative work by giving a short-term monopoly over certain uses of the work. This monopoly was granted to an individual or corporation by government. The government's power to grant a monopoly is corrupting. The biggest owners of intellectual property have sought to expand it well beyond any sensible rationale.

There are several types of intellectual property or, in other words, ownership of information, including copyright, patents, trademarks, trade secrets, design rights and plant breeders' rights. Copyright covers the expression of ideas such as in

29

writing, music and pictures. Patents cover inventions, such as new substances or articles and industrial processes. Trademarks are symbols associated with a good, service or company. Trade secrets cover confidential business information. Design rights cover different ways of presenting the outward appearance of things. Plant breeders' rights grant ownership of novel, distinct and stable plant varieties that are "invented."

The type of property that is familiar to most people is physical objects. People own clothes, cars, houses and land. But there has always been a big problem with owning ideas. Exclusive use or control of ideas or the way they are expressed doesn't make nearly as much sense as the ownership of physical objects.

Many physical objects can only be used by one person at a time. If one person wears a pair of shoes, no one else can wear them at the same time. (The person who wears them often owns them, but not always.) This is not true of intellectual property. Ideas can be copied over and over, but the person who had the original copy still has full use of it. Suppose you write a poem. Even if a million other people have copies and read the poem, you can still read the poem yourself. In other words, more than one person can use an idea—a poem, a mathematical formula, a tune, a letter—without reducing other people's use of the idea. Shoes and poems are fundamentally different in this respect.

Technological developments have made it cheaper and easier to make copies of information. Printing was a great advance: it eliminated the need for hand copying of documents. Photocopying and computers have made it even easier to make copies of written documents. Photography and sound recordings have done the same for visual and audio material. The ability to protect intellectual property is being undermined by technology. Yet there is a strong push to expand the scope of ownership of information.

This chapter outlines the case against intellectual property. I begin by mentioning some of the problems arising from ownership of information. Then I turn to weaknesses in its standard justifications. Next is an overview of problems with the so-called "marketplace of ideas," which has important links with intellectual property. Finally, I outline some alternatives to intellectual property and some possible strategies for moving towards them.

Problems with intellectual property

Governments generate large quantities of information. They produce statistics on population, figures on economic production and health, texts of laws and regulations, and vast numbers of reports. The generation of this information is paid for through taxation and, therefore, it might seem that it should be available to any member of the public. But in some countries, such as Britain and Australia, governments claim copyright in their own legislation and sometimes court decisions. Technically, citizens would need permission to copy their own laws. On the other hand, some government-generated information, especially in the US, is turned over to corporations that then sell it to whomever can pay. Publicly funded information is "privatised" and thus not freely available.[1]

The idea behind patents is that the fundamentals of an invention are made public while the inventor for a limited time has the exclusive right to make, use or sell the invention. But there are quite a few cases in which patents have been used to suppress innovation.[2] Companies may take out a patent, or buy someone else's patent, in order to inhibit others from applying the ideas. From its beginning in 1875, the US company AT&T collected patents in order to ensure its monopoly on telephones. It slowed down the introduction of radio for some 20 years. In a similar fashion, General Electric used control of patents to retard the

---

[1] Dorothy Nelkin, *Science as Intellectual Property: Who Controls Research?* (New York: Macmillan, 1984).

[2] Richard Dunford, "The suppression of technology as a strategy for controlling resource dependence," *Administrative Science Quarterly*, Vol. 32, 1987, pp. 512-525.

introduction of fluorescent lights, which were a threat to its sales of incandescent lights. Trade secrets are another way to suppress technological development. Trade secrets are protected by law but, unlike patents, do not have to be published openly. They can be overcome legitimately by independent development or reverse engineering.

Biological information can now be claimed as intellectual property. US courts have ruled that genetic sequences can be patented, even when the sequences are found "in nature," so long as some artificial means are involved in isolating them. This has led companies to race to take out patents on numerous genetic codes. In some cases, patents have been granted covering all transgenic forms of an entire species, such as soybeans or cotton, causing enormous controversy and sometimes reversals on appeal. One consequence is a severe inhibition on research by non-patent holders. Another consequence is that transnational corporations are patenting genetic materials found in Third World plants and animals, so that some Third World peoples actually have to pay to use seeds and other genetic materials that have been freely available to them for centuries.

More generally, intellectual property is one more way for rich countries to extract wealth from poor countries. Given the enormous exploitation of poor peoples built into the world trade system, it would only seem fair for ideas produced in rich countries to be provided at no cost to poor countries. Yet in the GATT negotiations, representatives of rich countries, especially the US, have insisted on strengthening intellectual property rights.[3] Surely there is no better indication that intellectual

---

3 Peter Drahos, "Global property rights in information: the story of TRIPS at the GATT," *Prometheus,* Vol. 13, No. 1, June 1995, pp. 6-19; Surendra J. Patel, "Intellectual property rights in the Uruguay Round: a disaster for the South?" *Economic and Political Weekly,* Vol. 24, No. 18, 6 May 1989, pp. 978-993; Darrell A. Posey and Graham Dutfield, *Beyond Intellectual Property: Toward Traditional Rights for Indigenous Peoples and Local Communities* (Ottawa: International Development Research Centre, 1996).

property is primarily of value to those who are already powerful and wealthy.

The potential financial returns from intellectual property are said to provide an incentive for individuals to create. In practice, though, most creators do not actually gain much benefit from intellectual property. Independent inventors are frequently ignored or exploited. When employees of corporations and governments have an idea worth protecting, it is usually copyrighted or patented by the organisation, not the employee. Since intellectual property can be sold, it is usually the rich and powerful who benefit. The rich and powerful, it should be noted, seldom contribute much intellectual labour to the creation of new ideas.

These problems—privatisation of government information, suppression of patents, ownership of genetic information and information not owned by the true creator—are symptoms of a deeper problem with the whole idea of intellectual property. Unlike goods, there are no physical obstacles to providing an abundance of ideas. (Indeed, the bigger problem may be an oversupply of ideas.) Intellectual property is an attempt to create an artificial scarcity in order to give rewards to a few at the expense of the many. Intellectual property aggravates inequality. It fosters competitiveness over information and ideas, whereas cooperation makes much more sense. In the words of Peter Drahos, researcher on intellectual property, "Intellectual property is a form of private sovereignty over a primary good—information."[4]

Here are some examples of the abuse of power that has resulted from the power to grant sovereignty over information.

• The neem tree is used in India in the areas of medicine, toiletries, contraception, timber, fuel and agriculture. Its uses

---

[4] Peter Drahos, "Decentring communication: the dark side of intellectual property," in Tom Campbell and Wojciech Sadurski (eds.), *Freedom of Communication* (Aldershot: Dartmouth, 1994), pp. 249-279, at p. 274.

have been developed over many centuries but never patented. Since the mid 1980s, US and Japanese corporations have taken out over a dozen patents on neem-based materials. In this way, collective local knowledge developed by Indian researchers and villagers has been expropriated by outsiders who have added very little to the process.[5]

• Charles M. Gentile is a US photographer who for a decade had made and sold artistic posters of scenes in Cleveland, Ohio. In 1995 he made a poster of the I. M. Pei building, which housed the new Rock and Roll Hall of Fame and Museum. This time he got into trouble. The museum sued him for infringing the trademark that it had taken out on its own image. If buildings can be registered as trademarks, then every painter, photographer and film-maker might have to seek permission and pay fees before using the images in their art work. This is obviously contrary to the original justification for intellectual property, which is to encourage the production of artistic works.

• Prominent designer Victor Papanek writes: "… there is something basically wrong with the whole concept of patents and copyrights. If I design a toy that provides therapeutic exercise for handicapped children, then I think it is unjust to delay the release of the design by a year and a half, going through a patent application. I feel that ideas are plentiful and cheap, and it is wrong to make money from the needs of others. I have been very lucky in persuading many of my students to accept this view. Much of what you will find as design examples throughout this book has never been patented. In fact, quite the opposite strategy prevails: in many cases students and I have made measured drawings of, say, a play environment for blind children, written a description of how to build it simply, and then

---

5 Vandana Shiva and Radha Holla-Bhar, "Intellectual piracy and the neem tree," *Ecologist,* Vol. 23, No. 6, 1993, pp. 223-227.

mimeographed drawings and all. If any agency, anywhere, will write in, my students will send them all the instructions free of charge."[6]

• In 1980, a book entitled *Documents on Australian Defence and Foreign Policy 1968-1975* was published by George Munster and Richard Walsh. It reproduced many secret government memos, briefings and other documents concerning Australian involvement in the Vietnam war, events leading up to the Indonesian invasion of East Timor, and other issues. Exposure of this material deeply embarrassed the Australian government. In an unprecedented move, the government issued an interim injunction, citing both the Crimes Act and the Copyright Act. The books, just put on sale, were impounded. Print runs of two major newspapers with extracts from the book were also seized.

The Australian High Court ruled that the Crimes Act did not apply, but that the material was protected by copyright held by the government. Thus copyright, set up to encourage artistic creation, was used to suppress dissemination of documents for whose production copyright was surely no incentive. Later, Munster and Walsh produced a book using summaries and short quotes in order to present the information.[7]

• Scientology is a religion in which only certain members at advanced stages of enlightenment have access to special information, which is secret to others. Scientology has long been controversial, with critics maintaining that it exploits members. Some critics, including former Scientologists, have put secret documents from advanced stages on the Internet. In response, church officials invoked copyright. Police have raided homes of critics, seizing computers, disks and other equipment. This is all

---

[6] Victor Papanek, *Design for the Real World: Human Ecology and Social Change* (London: Thames and Hudson, 1985, 2nd edition), p. xi.

[7] George Munster, *Secrets of State: A Detailed Assessment of the Book They Banned* (Australia: Walsh & Munster, 1982).

rather curious, since the stated purpose of copyright is not to hide information but rather to stimulate production of new ideas.[8]

The following examples show that the uncertainty of intellectual property law encourages ambit claims that seem to be somewhat plausible. Some targets of such claims give in for economic reasons.

• Ashleigh Brilliant is a "professional epigrammatist." He creates and copyrights thousands of short sayings, such as "Fundamentally, there may be no basis for anything." When he finds someone who has "used" one of his epigrams, he contacts them demanding a payment for breach of copyright. Television journalist David Brinkley wrote a book, *Everyone is Entitled to My Opinion*, the title of which he attributed to a friend of his daughter. Brilliant contacted Brinkley about copyright violation. Random House, Brinkley's publisher, paid Brilliant $1000 without contesting the issue, perhaps because it would have cost more than this to contest it.[9]

• Lawyer Robert Kunstadt has proposed that athletes could patent their sporting innovations, such as the "Fosbury flop" invented by high jumper Dick Fosbury. This might make a lot of money for a few stars. It would also cause enormous disputes. Athletes already have a tremendous incentive to innovate if it helps their performance. Patenting of basketball moves or choreography steps would serve mainly to limit the uptake of innovations and would mainly penalise those with fewer resources to pay royalties.

• The US National Basketball Association has sued in court for the exclusive right to transmit the scores of games as they are in

---

8   Wendy M. Grossman, "alt.scientology.war," *Wired,* Vol. 3, No. 12, December 1995, pp. 172-177, 248-252.

9   David D. Kirkpatrick, "Brilliant minds may think alike, but Brilliant lines can cost you," *Wall Street Journal,* 27 January 1997, p. B1.

progress. It had one success but lost on appeal.[10]

• A Scottish newspaper, *The Shetland Times*, went to court to stop an online news service from making a hypertext link to its web site. If hypertext links made without permission were made illegal, this would undermine the World Wide Web.[11]

These examples show that intellectual property has become a means for exerting power in ways quite divorced from its original aim—promoting the creation and use of new ideas.

Critique of standard justifications

Edwin C. Hettinger has provided an insightful critique of the main arguments used to justify intellectual property, so it is worthwhile summarising his analysis.[12] He begins by noting the obvious argument against intellectual property, namely that sharing intellectual objects still allows the original possessor to use them. Therefore, the burden of proof should lie on those who argue for intellectual property.

The first argument for intellectual property is that people are entitled to the results of their labour. Hettinger's response is that not all the value of intellectual products is due to labour. Nor is the value of intellectual products due to the work of a single labourer, or any small group. Intellectual products are social products.

Suppose you have written an essay or made an invention. Your intellectual work does not exist in a social vacuum. It would not have been possible without lots of earlier work—both

---

10 Lance Rose, "Technical foul: the NBA double dribbles on intellectual property," *Wired*, Vol. 5, No. 1, January 1997, p. 96.

11 Rob Edwards, "Scottish court case could unravel the Web," *New Scientist*, 16 November 1996, p. 5.

12 Edwin C. Hettinger, "Justifying intellectual property," *Philosophy and Public Affairs*, Vol. 18, No. 1, Winter 1989, pp. 31-52, quotes at pp. 39 and 42. See also David Vaver, "Intellectual property today: of myths and paradoxes," *Canadian Bar Review*, Vol. 69, No. 1, March 1990, pp. 98-128.

intellectual and nonintellectual—by many other people. This includes your teachers and parents. It includes the earlier authors and inventors who provided the foundation for your contribution. It also includes the many people who discussed and used ideas and techniques, at both theoretical and practical levels, and provided a cultural foundation for your contribution. It includes the people who built printing presses, laid telephone cables, built roads and buildings and in many other ways contributed to the "construction" of society. Many other people could be mentioned. The point is that any piece of intellectual work is always built on and is inconceivable without the prior work of numerous people.

Hettinger points out that the earlier contributors to the development of ideas are not present. Today's contributor therefore cannot validly claim full credit.

Is the market value of a piece of an intellectual product a reasonable indicator of a person's contribution? Certainly not. As noted by Hettinger and as will be discussed in the next section, markets only work once property rights have been established, so it is circular to argue that the market can be used to measure intellectual contributions. Hettinger summarises this point in this fashion: "The notion that a laborer is naturally entitled as a matter of right to receive the market value of her product is a myth. To what extent individual laborers should be allowed to receive the market value of their products is a question of social policy."

A related argument is that people have a right to possess and personally use what they develop. Hettinger's response is that this doesn't show that they deserve market values, nor that they should have a right to prevent others from using the invention.

A second major argument for intellectual property is that people *deserve* property rights because of their labour. This brings up the general issue of what people deserve, a topic that has been analysed by philosophers. Their usual conclusions go against what many people think is "common sense." Hettinger says that a fitting reward for labour should be proportionate to the person's effort, the risk taken and moral considerations. This sounds all right—but it is not proportionate to the value of the results of the labour, whether assessed through markets or by other criteria. This is because the value of intellectual work is affected by things not controlled by the worker, including luck and natural talent. Hettinger says "A person who is born with extraordinary natural talents, or who is extremely lucky, *deserves* nothing on the basis of these characteristics."

A musical genius like Mozart may make enormous contributions to society. But being born with enormous musical talents does not provide a justification for owning rights to musical compositions or performances. Likewise, the labour of developing a toy like Teenage Mutant Ninja Turtles that becomes incredibly popular does not provide a justification for owning rights to all possible uses of turtle symbols.

What about a situation where one person works hard at a task and a second person with equal talent works less hard? Doesn't the first worker deserve more reward? Perhaps so, but property rights do not provide a suitable mechanism for allocating rewards. The market can give great rewards to the person who successfully claims property rights for a discovery, with little or nothing for the person who just missed out.

A third argument for intellectual property is that private property is a means for promoting privacy and a means for personal autonomy. Hettinger responds that privacy is protected by not revealing information, not by owning it. Trade secrets cannot be defended on the grounds of privacy, because corporations are not individuals. As for personal autonomy, copyrights and patents aren't required for this.

A fourth argument is that rights in intellectual property are needed to promote the creation of more ideas. The idea is that intellectual property gives financial incentives to produce ideas. Hettinger thinks that this is the only decent argument for intellectual property. He is still somewhat sceptical, though. He notes that the whole argument is built on a contradiction, namely that in order to promote the development of ideas, it is necessary to reduce people's freedom to use them. Copyrights and patents may encourage new ideas and innovations, but they also restrict others from using them freely.

This argument for intellectual property cannot be resolved without further investigation. Hettinger says that there needs to be an investigation of how long patents and copyrights should be granted, to determine an optimum period for promoting intellectual work.

For the purposes of technological innovation, information becomes more valuable when augmented by new information: innovation is a collective process. If firms in an industry share information by tacit cooperation or open collaboration, this speeds innovation and reduces costs. Patents, which put information into the market and raise information costs, actually slow the innovative process.[13]

It should be noted that although the scale and pace of intellectual work has increased over the past few centuries, the duration of protection of intellectual property has not been reduced, as might be expected, but greatly increased. The US government did not recognise foreign copyrights for much of the 1800s. Where once copyrights were only for a period of a few decades, they now may be for the life of the author plus 70 years. In many countries, chemicals and pharmaceuticals were not patentable until recently. This suggests that even if intellectual property can be justified on the basis of fostering new ideas, this is not the driving force behind the present system of copyrights and patents. After all, few writers feel a greater incentive to write and publish just because their works are copyrighted for 70 years after they die, rather than just until they die.

Of various types of intellectual property, copyright is especially open for exploitation. Unlike patents, copyright is

---

13 Thomas Mandeville, *Understanding Novelty: Information, Technological Change, and the Patent System* (Norwood, NJ: Ablex, 1996).

granted without an application and lasts far longer. Originally designed to encourage literary and artistic work, it now applies to every memo and doodle and is more relevant to business than art. There is no need to encourage production of business correspondence, so why is copyright applied to it?[14]

Intellectual property is built around a fundamental tension: ideas are public but creators want private returns. To overcome this tension, a distinction developed between ideas and their expression. Ideas could not be copyrighted but their expression could. This peculiar distinction was tied to the romantic notion of the autonomous creator who somehow contributes to the common pool of ideas without drawing from it. This package of concepts apparently justified authors in claiming residual rights—namely copyright—in their ideas after leaving their hands, while not giving manual workers any rationale for claiming residual rights in *their* creations.[15] In practice, though, the idea-expression distinction is dubious and few of the major owners of intellectual property have the faintest resemblance to romantic creators.

The marketplace of ideas

The idea of intellectual property has a number of connections with the concept of the marketplace of ideas, a metaphor that is widely used in discussions of free speech. To delve a bit more deeply into the claim that intellectual property promotes development of new ideas, it is therefore helpful to scrutinise the concept of the marketplace of ideas.

The image conveyed by the marketplace of ideas is that ideas compete for acceptance in a market. As long as the competition is fair—which means that all ideas and contributors are permitted access to the marketplace—then good ideas will win

---

[14] David Vaver, "Rejuvenating copyright," *Canadian Bar Review,* Vol. 75, March 1996, pp. 69-80.

[15] James Boyle, *Shamans, Software, and Spleens: Law and the Social Construction of the Information Economy* (Cambridge, MA: Harvard University Press, 1996).

out over bad ones. Why? Because people will recognise the truth and value of good ideas. On the other hand, if the market is constrained, for example by some groups being excluded, then certain ideas cannot be tested and examined and successful ideas may not be the best ideas.

Logically, there is no reason why a marketplace of ideas has to be a marketplace of *owned* ideas: intellectual property cannot be strictly justified by the marketplace of ideas. But because the marketplace metaphor is an economic one, there is a strong tendency to link intellectual property with the marketplace of ideas. As discussed later, there is a link between these two concepts, but not in the way their defenders usually imagine.

There are plenty of practical examples of the failure of the marketplace of ideas. Groups that are stigmatised or that lack power seldom have their viewpoints presented. This includes ethnic minorities, prisoners, the unemployed, manual workers and radical critics of the status quo, among many others. Even when such groups organise themselves to promote their ideas, their views are often ignored while the media focus on their protests, as in the case of peace movement rallies and marches.

Demonstrably, good ideas do not always win out in the marketplace of ideas. To take one example, the point of view of workers is frequently just as worthy as that of employers. Yet there is an enormous imbalance in the presentation of their respective viewpoints in the media. One result is that quite a few ideas that happen to serve the interests of employers at the expense of workers—such as that the reason people don't have jobs is because they aren't trying hard enough to find them—are widely accepted although they are rejected by virtually all informed analysts.

There is a simple and fundamental reason for the failure of the marketplace of ideas: inequality, especially economic inequality.[16] Perhaps in a group of people sitting in a room

---

[16] C. Edwin Baker, *Human Liberty and Freedom of Speech* (New York: Oxford University Press, 1989).

discussing an issue, there is some prospect of a measured assessment of different ideas. But if these same people are isolated in front of their television sets, and one of them owns the television station, it is obvious that there is little basis for testing of ideas. The reality is that powerful and rich groups can promote their ideas with little chance of rebuttal from those with different perspectives. As described in chapter 2, the mass media are powerful enterprises that promote their own interests as well as those of governments and corporations.

In circumstances where participants are approximate equals, such as intellectual discussion among peers in an academic discipline, then the metaphor of competition of ideas has some value. But ownership of media or ideas is hardly a prerequisite for such discussion. It is the equality of power that is essential. To take one of many possible examples, when employees in corporations lack the freedom to speak openly without penalty they cannot be equal participants in discussions (see chapter 5).

Some ideas are good—in the sense of being valuable to society—but are unwelcome. Some are unwelcome to powerful groups, such as that governments and corporations commit horrific crimes or that there is a massive trade in technologies of torture and repression that needs to be stopped. Others are challenging to much of the population, such as that imprisonment does not reduce the crime rate or that financial rewards for good work on the job or grades for good schoolwork are counterproductive.[17] (Needless to say, individuals might disagree with the examples used here. The case does not rest on the examples themselves, but on the existence of some socially

---

[17] On these points, see respectively Jeffrey Ian Ross (ed.), *Controlling State Crime: An Introduction* (New York: Garland, 1995); Steve Wright, "The new technologies of political repression: a case for arms control?" *Philosophy and Social Action,* Vol. 17, Nos. 3-4, July-December 1991, pp. 31-62; Nils Christie, *Crime Control as Industry: Towards Gulags, Western Style* (London: Routledge, 1994, 2nd edition); Alfie Kohn, *Punished by Rewards: The Trouble with Gold Stars, Incentive Plans, A's, Praise, and other Bribes* (Boston: Houghton Mifflin, 1993).

valuable ideas that are unwelcome and marginalised.) The
marketplace of ideas simply does not work to treat such unwelcome ideas with the seriousness they deserve. The mass media
try to gain audiences by pleasing them, not by confronting them
with challenging ideas.[18]

The marketplace of ideas is often used to justify free speech.
The argument is that free speech is necessary in order for the
marketplace of ideas to operate: if some types of speech are
curtailed, certain ideas will not be available on the marketplace
and thus the best ideas will not succeed. This sounds plausible.
But it is possible to reject the marketplace of ideas while still
defending free speech on the grounds that it is essential to
human liberty.

If the marketplace of ideas doesn't work, what is the
solution? The usual view is that governments should intervene to
ensure that all groups have fair access to the media. But this
approach, based on promoting equality of opportunity, ignores
the fundamental problem of economic inequality. Even if
minority groups have some limited chance to present their views
in the mass media, this can hardly compensate for the massive
power of governments and corporations to promote their views.
In addition, it retains the role of the mass media as the central
mechanism for disseminating ideas. So-called reform proposals
either retain the status quo or introduce government censorship.

Underlying the market model is the idea of self-regulation:
the "free market" is supposed to operate without outside intervention and, indeed, to operate best when outside intervention is
minimised. In practice, even markets in goods do not operate
autonomously: the state is intimately involved in even the freest
of markets. In the case of the marketplace of ideas, the state is
involved both in shaping the market and in making it possible,
for example by promoting and regulating the mass media. The
world's most powerful state, the US, has been the driving force

---

[18] Robert M. Entman, *Democracy without Citizens: Media and the Decay of
American Politics* (New York: Oxford University Press, 1989).

behind the establishment of a highly protectionist system of intellectual property, using power politics at GATT, the General Agreement on Tariffs and Trade.

Courts may use the rhetoric of the marketplace of ideas but actually interpret the law to support the status quo. For example, speech is treated as free until it might actually have some consequences. Then it is curtailed when it allegedly presents a "clear and present danger," such as when peace activists expose information supposedly threatening to "national security". But speech without action is pointless. True liberty requires freedom to promote one's views in practice.[19] Powerful groups have the ability to do this. Courts only intervene when others try to do the same.

As in the case of trade generally, a property-based "free market" serves the interests of powerful producers. In the case of ideas, this includes governments and corporations plus intellectuals and professionals linked with universities, entertainment, journalism and the arts. Against such an array of intellectual opinion, it is very difficult for other groups, such as manual workers, to compete.[20] The marketplace of ideas is a biased and artificial market that mostly serves to fine-tune relations between elites and provide them with legitimacy.[21]

The implication of this analysis is that intellectual property cannot be justified on the basis of the marketplace of ideas. The utilitarian argument for intellectual property is that ownership is necessary to stimulate production of new ideas, because of the financial incentive. This financial incentive is supposed to come from the market, whose justification is the marketplace of ideas. If, as critics argue, the marketplace of ideas is flawed by the presence of economic inequality and, more fundamentally, is an

---

[19] Baker (see note 16).
[20] Benjamin Ginsberg, *The Captive Public: How Mass Media Promotes State Power* (New York: Basic Books, 1986).
[21] Stanley Ingber, "The marketplace of ideas: a legitimizing myth," *Duke Law Journal,* Vol. 1984, No. 1, February 1984, pp. 1-91.

artificial creation that serves powerful producers of ideas and legitimates the role of elites, then the case for intellectual property is unfounded. Intellectual property can only serve to aggravate the inequality on which it is built.

The alternative

The alternative to intellectual property is straightforward: intellectual products should not be owned. That means not owned by individuals, corporations, governments, or the community as common property. It means that ideas are available to be used by anyone who wants to.

One example of how this might operate is language, including the words, sounds and meaning systems with which we communicate every day. Spoken language is free for everyone to use. (Actually, corporations do control bits of language through trademarks and slogans.)

Another example is scientific knowledge. Scientists do research and then publish their results. A large proportion of scientific knowledge is public knowledge. There are some areas of science that are not public, such as classified military research. It is usually argued that the most dynamic parts of science are those with the least secrecy. Open ideas can be examined, challenged, modified and improved. To turn scientific knowledge into a commodity on the market, as is happening with genetic engineering, arguably inhibits science.

Few scientists complain that they do not own the knowledge they produce. Indeed, they are much more likely to complain when corporations or governments try to control dissemination of ideas. Most scientists receive a salary from a government, corporation or university. Their livelihoods do not depend on royalties from published work.

University scientists have the greatest freedom. The main reasons they do research are for the intrinsic satisfaction of investigation and discovery—a key motivation for many of the world's great scientists—and for recognition by their peers. To turn scientific knowledge into intellectual property would dampen the enthusiasm of many scientists for their work. However, as governments reduce their funding of universities, scientists and university administrations increasingly turn to patents as a source of income.

Language and scientific knowledge are not ideal; indeed, they are often used for harmful purposes. It is difficult to imagine, though, how turning them into property could make them better.

The case of science shows that vigorous intellectual activity is quite possible without intellectual property, and in fact that it may be vigorous precisely because information is not owned. But there are lots of areas that, unlike science, have long operated with intellectual property as a fact of life. What would happen without ownership of information? Many objections spring to mind.

Plagiarism

Many intellectual workers fear being plagiarised and many of them think that intellectual property provides protection against this. After all, without copyright, why couldn't someone put their name on your essay and publish it? Actually, copyright provides very little protection against plagiarism.[22] So-called "moral rights" of authors to be credited are backed by law in many countries but are an extremely cumbersome way of dealing with plagiarism.

Plagiarism means using the ideas of others without adequate acknowledgment. There are several types of plagiarism. One is plagiarism of ideas: someone takes your original idea and, using different expression, presents it as their own. Copyright provides no protection at all against this form of plagiarism. Another type of plagiarism is word-for-word plagiarism, where someone takes the words you've written—a book, an essay, a few paragraphs or even just a sentence—and, with or without minor modifications, presents them as their own. This sort of plagiarism *is* covered by

---

[22] Laurie Stearns, "Copy wrong: plagiarism, process, property, and the law," *California Law Review,* Vol. 80, No. 2, March 1992, pp. 513-553.

copyright—assuming that you hold the copyright. In many cases, copyright is held by the publisher, not the author.

In practice, plagiarism goes on all the time, in various ways and degrees,[23] and copyright law is hardly ever used against it. The most effective challenge to plagiarism is not legal action but publicity. At least among authors, plagiarism is widely condemned. For this reason, and because they seek to give credit where it's due, most writers do take care to avoid plagiarising.

There is an even more fundamental reason why copyright provides no protection against plagiarism: the most common sort of plagiarism is built into social hierarchies. Government and corporate reports are released under the names of top bureaucrats who did not write them; politicians and corporate executives give speeches written by underlings. These are examples of a pervasive misrepresentation of authorship in which powerful figures gain credit for the work of subordinates.[24] Copyright, if it has any effect at all, reinforces rather than challenges this sort of institutionalised plagiarism.

Royalties

What about all the writers, inventors and others who depend for their livelihood on royalties? First, it should be mentioned that only a very few individuals make enough money from royalties to live on. For example, there are probably only a few hundred self-employed writers in the US.[25] Most of the rewards from intellectual property go to a few big companies. But the question is still a serious one for those intellectual workers who depend on royalties and other payments related to intellectual property.

---

[23] Thomas Mallon, *Stolen Words: Forays into the Origins and Ravages of Plagiarism* (New York: Ticknor and Fields, 1989); Ari Posner, "The culture of plagiarism," *The New Republic,* 18 April 1988, pp. 19-24.

[24] Brian Martin, "Plagiarism: a misplaced emphasis," *Journal of Information Ethics,* Vol. 3, No. 2, Fall 1994, pp. 36-47.

[25] Vaver, 1990 (see note 12).

The alternative in this case is some reorganisation of the economic system. Those few currently dependent on royalties could instead receive a salary, grant or bursary, just as most scientists do.

Getting rid of intellectual property would reduce the incomes of a few highly successful creative individuals, such as author Agatha Christie, composer Andrew Lloyd Webber and filmmaker Steven Spielberg. Publishers could reprint Christie's novels without permission, theatre companies could put on Webber's operas whenever they wished and Spielberg's films could be copied and screened anywhere. Jurassic Park and Lost World T-shirts, toys and trinkets could be produced at will. This would reduce the income of and, to some extent, the opportunities for artistic expression by these individuals. But there would be economic resources released: there would be more money available for other creators. Christie, Webber and Spielberg might be just as popular without intellectual property to channel money to them and their family enterprises.

The typical creative intellectual is actually worse off due to intellectual property. Consider an author who brings in a few hundred or even a few thousand dollars of royalty income per year. This is a tangible income, which creators value for its monetary and symbolic value. But this should be weighed against payments of royalties and monopoly profits when buying books, magazines, CDs and computer software.

Many of these costs are invisible. How many consumers, for example, realise how much they are paying for intellectual property when buying prescription medicines, paying for schools (through fees or taxes), buying groceries or listening to a piece of music on the radio? Yet in these and many other situations, costs are substantially increased due to intellectual property. Most of the extra costs go not to creators but to corporations and to bureaucratic overheads—such as patent offices and law firms—that are necessary to keep the system of intellectual property going.

Stimulating creativity

What about the incentive to create? Without the possibility of wealth and fame, what would stimulate creative individuals to produce works of genius? Actually, most creators and innovators are motivated by their own intrinsic interest, not by rewards. There is a large body of evidence showing, contrary to popular opinion, that rewards actually reduce the quality of work.[26] If the goal is better and more creative work, paying creators on a piecework basis, such as through royalties, is counterproductive.

In a society without intellectual property, creativity is likely to thrive. Most of the problems that are imagined to occur if there is no intellectual property—such as the exploitation of a small publisher that renounces copyright—are due to economic arrangements that maintain inequality. The soundest foundation for a society without intellectual property is greater economic and political equality. This means not just equality of opportunity, but equality of outcomes. This does not mean uniformity and does not mean levelling imposed from the top: it means freedom and diversity and a situation where people can get what they need but are not able to gain great power or wealth by exploiting the work of others. This is a big issue. Suffice it to say here that there are strong social and psychological arguments in favour of equality.[27]

Strategies for change

Intellectual property is supported by many powerful groups: the most powerful governments and the largest corporations. The mass media seem fully behind intellectual property, partly because media monopolies would be undercut if information were more freely copied and partly because the most influential journalists depend on syndication rights for their stories.

---

[26] Kohn (see note 17).

[27] John Baker, *Arguing for Equality* (London: Verso, 1987); Morton Deutsch, *Distributive Justice: A Social-psychological Perspective* (New Haven: Yale University Press, 1985); William Ryan, *Equality* (New York: Pantheon, 1981).

Perhaps just as important is the support for intellectual property from many small intellectual producers, including academics and freelance writers. Although the monetary returns to these intellectuals are seldom significant, they have been persuaded that they both need and deserve their small royalties. This is similar to the way that small owners of goods and land, such as homeowners, strongly defend the system of private property, whose main beneficiaries are the very wealthy who own vast enterprises based on many other people's labour. Intellectuals are enormous consumers as well as producers of intellectual work. A majority would probably be better off financially without intellectual property, since they wouldn't have to pay as much for other people's work.

Another problem in developing strategies is that it makes little sense to challenge intellectual property in isolation. If we simply imagine intellectual property being abolished but the rest of the economic system unchanged, then many objections can be made. Challenging intellectual property must involve the development of methods to support creative individuals.

Change thinking

Talking about "intellectual property" implies an association with physical property. Instead, it is better to talk about monopolies granted by governments, for example "monopoly privilege." This gives a better idea of what's going on and so helps undermine the legitimacy of the process. Associated with this could be an appeal to free market principles, challenging the barriers to trade in ideas imposed by monopolies granted to copyright and patent holders.

As well, a connection should be forged with ideals of free speech. Rather than talk of intellectual property in terms of property and trade, it should be talked about in terms of speech and its impediments. Controls over genetic information should be talked about in terms of public health and social welfare rather than property.

The way that an issue is framed makes an enormous difference to the legitimacy of different positions. Once intellectual property is undermined in the minds of many citizens, it will become far easier to topple its institutional supports.

Expose the costs

It can cost a lot to set up and operate a system of intellectual property. This includes patent offices, legislation, court cases, agencies to collect fees and much else. There is a need for research to calculate and expose these costs as well as the transfers of money between different groups and countries. A middle-ranking country from the First World, such as Australia, pays far more for intellectual property—mostly to the US—than it receives. Once the figures are available and understood, this will aid in reducing the legitimacy of the world intellectual property system.[28]

Reproduce protected works

From the point of view of intellectual property, this is called "piracy." (This is a revealing term, considering that such language is seldom used when, for example, a boss takes credit for a subordinate's work or when a Third World intellectual is recruited to a First World position. In each case, investments in intellectual work made by an individual or society are exploited by a different individual or society with more power.) This happens every day when people photocopy copyrighted articles, tape copyrighted music, or duplicate copyrighted software. It is precisely because illegal copying is so easy and so common that big governments and corporations have mounted offensives to promote intellectual property rights.

Unfortunately, illegal copying is not a very good strategy against intellectual property, any more than stealing goods is a

---

[28] These two strategies are proposed by Peter Drahos, "Thinking strategically about intellectual property rights," paper prepared for the Forum of Parliamentarians on Intellectual Property and the National Working Group on Patent Laws, 1996.

way to challenge ownership of physical property. Theft of any sort implicitly accepts the existing system of ownership. By trying to hide the copying and avoiding penalties, the copiers appear to accept the legitimacy of the system.

Openly refuse to cooperate with intellectual property

This is far more powerful than illicit copying. The methods of nonviolent action can be used here, including noncooperation, boycotts and setting up alternative institutions. By being open about the challenge, there is a much greater chance of focussing attention on the issues at stake and creating a dialogue. By being principled in opposition, and being willing to accept penalties for civil disobedience to laws on intellectual property, there is a much greater chance of winning over third parties. If harsh penalties are applied to those who challenge intellectual property, this could produce a backlash of sympathy. Once mass civil disobedience to intellectual property laws occurs, it will be impossible to stop.

Something like that is already occurring. Because photocopying of copyrighted works is so common, there is seldom any attempt to enforce the law against small violators—to do so would alienate too many people. Copyright authorities therefore seek other means of collecting revenues from intellectual property, such as payments by institutions based on library copies.

Already there is mass discontent in India over the impact of the world intellectual property regime and patenting of genetic materials, with rallies of hundreds of thousands of farmers.[29] If this scale of protest could be combined with other actions that undermine the legitimacy of intellectual property, the entire system could be challenged.

---

[29] The magazine *Third World Resurgence* has regular reports on this issue. See for example Martin Khor, "A worldwide fight against biopiracy and patents on life," *Third World Resurgence,* No. 63, November 1995, pp. 9-11, and the special issues on patenting of life: No. 57, May 1995 and No. 84, August 1997.

Promote non-owned information

A good example is public domain software, which is computer software that is made available free to anyone who wants it. The developers of "freeware" gain satisfaction out of their intellectual work and out of providing a service to others. The Free Software Foundation has spearheaded the development and promotion of freeware. It "is dedicated to eliminating restrictions on people's right to use, copy, modify and redistribute computer programs" by encouraging people to develop and use free software.

A suitable alternative to copyright is shareright. A piece of freeware might be accompanied by the notice, "You may reproduce this material if your recipients may also reproduce it." This encourages copiers but refuses any of them copyright.

The Free Software Foundation has come up with another approach, called "copyleft." The Foundation states, "The simplest way to make a program free is to put it in the public domain, uncopyrighted. But this permits proprietary modified versions, which deny others the freedom to redistribute and modify; such versions undermine the goal of giving freedom to all users. To prevent this, 'copyleft' uses copyright in a novel manner. Typically copyrights take away freedoms; copyleft preserves them. It is a legal instrument that requires those who pass on a program to include the rights to use, modify, and redistribute the code; the code and the freedoms become legally inseparable."[30] Until copyright is eliminated or obsolete, innovations such as copyleft are necessary to avoid exploitation of those who want to make their work available to others.

Develop principles to deal with credit for intellectual work

This is important even if credit is not rewarded financially. This would include guidelines for not misrepresenting another

---

[30] *GNU's Bulletin,* January 1995 (Free Software Foundation, 59 Temple Place, Suite 330, Boston MA 02111-1307, USA; gnu@prep.ai.mit.edu). See http://www.gnu.org/ for the latest description.

person's work. Intellectual property gives the appearance of stopping unfair appropriation of ideas although the reality is quite different. If intellectual property is to be challenged, people need to be reassured that misappropriation of ideas will not become a big problem.

More fundamentally, it needs to be recognised that intellectual work is inevitably a collective process. No one has totally original ideas: ideas are always built on the earlier contributions of others. (That's especially true of this chapter!) Furthermore, culture—which makes ideas possible—is built not just on intellectual contributions but also on practical and material contributions, including the rearing of families and construction of buildings. Intellectual property is theft, sometimes in part from an individual creator but always from society as a whole.

In a more cooperative society, credit for ideas would not be such a contentious matter. Today, there are vicious disputes between scientists over who should gain credit for a discovery. This is because scientists' careers and, more importantly, their reputations, depend on credit for ideas. In a society with less hierarchy and greater equality, intrinsic motivation and satisfaction would be the main returns from contributing to intellectual developments. This is quite compatible with everything that is known about human nature.[31] The system of ownership encourages groups to put special interests above general interests. Sharing information is undoubtedly the most efficient way to allocate productive resources. The less there is to gain from credit for ideas, the more likely people are to share ideas rather than worry about who deserves credit for them.

* * *

For most book publishers, publishing an argument against intellectual property raises a dilemma. If the work is copyrighted as

---

[31] Alfie Kohn, *The Brighter Side of Human Nature: Altruism and Empathy in Everyday Life* (New York: Basic Books, 1990).

usual, this clashes with the argument against copyright. On the other hand, if the work is not copyrighted, then unrestrained copying might undermine sales. It's worth reflecting on this dilemma as it applies to this book.

It is important to keep in mind the wider goal of challenging the corruptions of information power. Governments and large corporations are particularly susceptible to these corruptions. They should be the first targets in developing a strategy against intellectual property.

Freedom Press is not a typical publisher. It has been publishing anarchist writings since 1886, including books, magazines, pamphlets and leaflets. Remarkably, neither authors nor editors have ever been paid for their work. Freedom Press is concerned with social issues and social change, not with material returns to anyone involved in the enterprise.

Because it is a small publisher, Freedom Press would be hard pressed to enforce its claims to copyright even if it wanted to. Those who sympathise with the aims of Freedom Press and who would like to reproduce some of its publications therefore should consider practical rather than legal issues. Would the copying be on such a scale as to undermine Freedom Press's limited sales? Does the copying give sufficient credit to Freedom Press so as to encourage further sales? Is the copying for commercial or noncommercial purposes?

In answering such questions, it makes sense to ask Freedom Press. This applies whether the work is copyright or not. If asking is not feasible, or the copying is of limited scale, then good judgement should be used. In my opinion, using one chapter—especially this chapter!—for nonprofit purposes should normally be okay.

So in the case of Freedom Press, the approach should be to negotiate in good faith and to use good judgement in minor or urgent cases. Negotiation and good judgement of this sort will be necessary in any society that moves beyond intellectual property.

4

Antisurveillance

Surveillance, a serious and growing issue, is basically a problem of unequal power. The usual reform solutions, such as codes of professional ethics, laws and regulations, give only an illusion of protection. Another approach is to promote grassroots challenges to surveillance either through disruption or by replacing social institutions that create a demand for surveillance. A long-term programme for institutional change helps in choosing directions for antisurveillance campaigns.

Today, information about citizens is collected by dozens of corporations and government bureaucracies, including police, taxation departments, marketing firms and banks. Cameras and listening devices are commonplace. Technologies to automatically recognise people's faces or hands are being refined.

So central is surveillance that countries such as Sweden, Germany and the United States have been called "surveillance societies." Yet few people are enthusiastic about the increased capacity of large organisations to collect information about themselves. Opinion surveys regularly show that most people attach great value·to their own privacy—though not always to other people's privacy. However, concern about invasions of privacy has not led to a mass movement against surveillance. Privacy campaigner Simon Davies notes that activist privacy groups are folding up or losing energy, though citizen action is desperately needed.

So far, the main responses to the threat of surveillance—codes of professional ethics, laws and regulations—have given only an illusion of protection. These responses may be adequate in some circumstances, but they don't address the driving forces behind surveillance: power, profit and control. Codes of ethics seem to have made little impact, while laws and regulations are regularly flouted or made obsolete by technological change.

There is another approach, which has received relatively little attention: to challenge and replace the social structures that promote surveillance. My aim in this chapter is to outline a radical antisurveillance agenda. It is an exercise in thinking about massive changes in the organisation of society and especially in the distribution of power. Of course, this can be considered "unrealistic" in the sense that such changes will be opposed by powerful groups and thus be difficult to achieve. But envisioning alternatives has the advantage of indicating directions for today's campaigns that will make some contribution to long-term change. What is actually unrealistic is to imagine that the problem of surveillance can be addressed by band-aid methods.

First, I give an overview of the problem and discuss surveillance as a problem of unequal power. Next, I describe the failure of reform solutions—that is, solutions implemented by powerful groups—and the limitations of technical fixes. Then I describe two grassroots programmes against surveillance, a "disruption programme" and an "institutional change programme." The disruption programme is one designed to disrupt the process of surveillance, for example by corrupting databases. The institutional change programme is built around challenging and replacing social institutions that create a demand for surveillance. In conclusion, I argue that the institutional change programme provides help in choosing directions for present-day antisurveillance campaigns.

The problem[1]

Surveillance is not a new problem. The lack of privacy in small, intimate communities is notorious. What is new are invasions of privacy by large, remote organisations. There are two main factors here. First is the rise of large-scale bureaucratic organisations, both corporations and government bodies, in the past few hundred years. Second is the development of technologies for communicating at a distance and for collecting and processing large quantities of information. Computers and telecommunications are central here.

The capacities for collecting data about individuals are epitomised by the computerised database. There are thousands of such databases, including police files, military records, welfare files, marketing lists, taxation files, medical records and credit listings. Most of these are compiled when we fill out forms, such as a census form, an application for a loan, a registration for a hospital visit, enrolment at a school, an application for an automobile licence or a subscription to a magazine. Further

---

[1] See, among others, David Burnham, *The Rise of the Computer State* (London: Weidenfeld and Nicolson, 1983); Duncan Campbell and Steve Connor, *On the Record: Surveillance, Computers and Privacy—The Inside Story* (London: Michael Joseph, 1986); Ann Cavoukian and Don Tapscott, *Who Knows: Safeguarding Your Privacy in a Networked World* (New York: McGraw-Hill, 1997); Roger A. Clarke, "Information technology and dataveillance," *Communications of the ACM,* Vol. 31, No. 5, May 1988, pp. 498-512; Simon Davies, *Monitor: Extinguishing Privacy on the Information Superhighway* (Sydney: Pan Macmillan, 1996); David H. Flaherty, *Protecting Privacy in Surveillance Societies: The Federal Republic of Germany, Sweden, France, Canada, and the United States* (Chapel Hill: University of North Carolina Press, 1989); Oscar H. Gandy, Jr., *The Panoptic Sort: A Political Economy of Personal Information* (Boulder, CO: Westview, 1993); Kenneth C. Laudon, *Dossier Society: Values Choices in the Design of National Information Systems* (New York: Columbia University Press, 1986); David Lyon, *The Electronic Eye: The Rise of Surveillance Society* (Cambridge: Polity Press, 1994); Gary T. Marx, *Undercover: Police Surveillance in America* (Berkeley: University of California Press, 1988); James Rule, Doug McAdam, Linda Stearns and David Uglow, *The Politics of Privacy* (New York: Elsevier, 1980).

information is added by banks (every deposit or withdrawal), doctors (each visit to a hospital), teachers (grades for all courses), and many others.

The capacity to manipulate databases on a computer allows invasions of privacy never imagined in earlier days. For example, many telephone directories are now available in computerised form. It is a simple matter to insert a telephone number and obtain the name and address. Marketeers can put in the name of a street and obtain a listing of the names and phone numbers of the people living there. These so-called "reverse telephone directories" allow going from numbers or addresses to names, something not previously anticipated in compiling directories.

Police sitting in their patrol car can access computerised police files remotely. They can key in the licence number of a car that is being driven dangerously, whose occupants "look suspicious" or that is parked near a political meeting. They can receive information about the car owner's police record, and they can add information to the owner's file.

Databases are far from secure. Getting access to "confidential" information is often a simple matter of connections and money. Private investigators obtain information about credit ratings, police records, tax payments and the like by ringing up "friends" in the relevant agency and making an appropriate payment. This practice is illegal but commonplace.

Lack of security is only one problem. Another is inaccuracy. In one case, police repeatedly arrested a man for a crime he didn't commit; the real criminal had stolen his identification documents. In another case, a woman was repeatedly denied rental accommodation; it turned out that she was recorded on a credit-rating database as a bad risk due to defaulting from payments, although it was the owner who was to blame. Surveillance can be a risk even for those who are honest and have nothing to hide.

Individual databases are powerful tools. When they are linked to each other, enormous new potentials are created. For example, taxation records can be linked automatically to records of divorced parents who have failed to maintain court-specified child support payments. It is then a simple matter to extract the payments in the process of assessing income tax. The beauty of this approach, from the administrator's point of view, is that the defaulter cannot escape by leaving town, as the surveillance operates on a national or even international scale.

The computer records of a driver, stopped for speeding, can be checked and a demand made for payment of parking fines—or library fines. Lists of subscribers to magazines are commonly sold to other organisations; the subscribers then become targets for sales messages.

Some telephone systems allow the telephone number of the caller to be registered by the receiver in a display. It is also possible to automatically record the caller's number. A company can offer a free gift to anyone ringing a particular number and thus obtain a listing of all numbers that ring up. The numbers then can be used for direct telephone solicitations. Telephone marketing can be partly automated, with a computer dialling the number and conducting at least the first part of the conversation.

With old-style printed files, a definite decision was required to search out information about someone in particular. A bank teller used to need a reason or suspicion before pulling out the file for a customer at the counter. Doing this for everyone would simply take too long. Computerised files allow routine checking. The system can be designed so that every time someone comes into a bank for a deposit or withdrawal, their file is retrieved in a matter of seconds—with, for example, the information that they are overdue on a loan repayment. What this means is that information is automatically checked: everyone is under suspicion.

Just as computers can store and manipulate information in ways impossible previously, so other new technologies make it possible to collect ever more detailed and personal information about individuals. Bugging devices have been around a long time, but they are smaller, harder to detect and provide better quality transmissions than ever before. Video cameras are apparent in many shops, but there are also many that are not so apparent, for example hidden inside lights.

For the serious snooper with enough money, the technological capabilities are awesome. Nightscopes can detect infrared radiation in order to see in the dark. Sensitive sound receivers can listen in to conversations from outside a building, by deciphering the vibrations on a window pane in a room in which people are speaking. Computer-to-computer communications can be intercepted and decoded. The information on a computer screen can be picked up in a nearby room from emitted radiation, without any direct electric connection. (On the other hand, not all fancy new technologies are as effective as promotional material may assert or fearful targets may believe.)

Some of the opportunities for surveillance are open to anyone. For example, it is easy to use a radio receiver to listen in on a neighbour's conversations on a cordless telephone.

In the future, surveillance is likely to become ever more intrusive and unavoidable. Surveillance cameras are being used in more and more public and private places. One development under way is tiny recorders and transmitters that can be transported on miniature flying craft that could be piloted into a person's back yard. Eventually they might be reduced to the size of insects that could enter a room and record whatever is said or done. This would be a "bug" in both senses of the word.

It is in the workplace where surveillance has long been most intense and where the new technologies are "employed" to greatest effect. Word processors have their keystrokes monitored, and indeed computers are regularly set up to monitor any routine process. Open or hidden cameras are commonplace. Beyond this, employers are seeking deeper knowledge about their workers. Psychological tests are often used to select workers or, more commonly, to rule them out. Physical features are under scrutiny too, especially in the United States, where blood and urine tests are increasingly demanded as a condition of employment. Whether the aim is to screen out workers with communicable diseases (such as AIDS) or to detect users of illegal drugs, the effect is ever greater exposure of previously private information about individuals.

Gary Marx, author of some of the most insightful studies of surveillance, points out that new technologies overcome most of the natural barriers that protected privacy in the past.[2] Surveillance technologies can operate at a distance, penetrate darkness and go through physical barriers, as in the case of various listening devices. Surveillance is harder to detect than ever before, whether through hidden cameras or remote listening devices. Surveillance requires less labour than before, since technology now can do much of the work. For example, telephone taps used to require tedious listening of all conversations; now computers with voice recognition can be used to signal the presence of "trigger" words such as "bomb."

Surveillance has long been a central feature of institutions of social control, notably prisons and mental institutions. New technologies allow this control to be extended into the community. In a number of countries, people can serve sentences at home, so-called "home detention." Typically, they wear electronic bracelets or anklets which communicate with a central computer, which monitors their nearness to the house. One of the arguments for such alternatives to prison is that they would reduce prison populations, but the reality is that an ever-larger number of people may be caught in the net of the criminal justice system.[3]

Surveillance and power

The above examples of surveillance today give an idea of the scope of the problem. How is the problem to be understood?

---

[2] Gary T. Marx, "The iron fist and the velvet glove: totalitarian potentials within democratic structures," in James F. Short, Jr. (ed.), *The Social Fabric: Dimensions and Issues* (Beverly Hills: Sage, 1986), pp. 135-162.

[3] Stanley Cohen, *Visions of Social Control: Crime, Punishment and Classification* (Cambridge: Polity Press, 1985).

There are various perspectives available. For my purposes, it is useful to analyse surveillance as a cause and consequence of inequality of power. The key issue is the surveillance of the less powerful by the more powerful.

The word "surveillance" has connotations of nastiness, but a little reflection reveals that keeping a close watch on others is not inherently bad. For example, it makes sense to keep a close watch on small children to make sure that they do not get hurt. The same applies to the sick and infirm. Many people appreciate someone watching out for them when they are doing something that is potentially risky, such as swimming in the sea or climbing a tall ladder. These are examples of "surveillance" which can be most welcomed.

When people live together, they observe a lot about each other, and this can be considered a type of surveillance. It occurs in families, among friends, and in close-knit communities. Some of the attention in these circumstances may be resented, but much of it is an inevitable consequence of living as a member of a community. It can be a joy to see friends along the street or in a restaurant or to have them visit your home, even though they thereby know more about what you are doing at any particular time.

Most people are not concerned about "surveillance" in such situations. Why not? In some of the cases, such as meeting friends, there is both a mutual agreement to participate and a rough equality of power. But in the case of a parent and a small child, there is an enormous difference in power and no real possibility of informed consent on the child's part. What makes the close watching in this situation acceptable is the trust implicit in the relationship: the trust that the parent will look after the child. (Of course, this trust may be violated, as when a parent beats or sexually abuses a child. Such actions justify intervention by others, whether family, friends or the state.)

What is normally called surveillance then applies to cases when either there is a substantial power difference or a lack of a trust relationship, or both. A large powerful organisation that collects data on individuals is a typical case. The organisation is able to collect data because it is powerful and becomes more powerful because of the data.

Is the fundamental problem the surveillance or the inequality in power? They are linked, so perhaps these two things can't be easily distinguished.

Note that I have couched this discussion in terms of surveillance and power rather than in terms of privacy and individual rights. Many of the writers in this area focus on privacy, assuming that there is a right to privacy and that violations of individual privacy must be weighed up against other competing values (such as increasing efficiency or stopping crime). This language of privacy and rights is typical of liberalism. It assumes that individuals are isolated entities who have agreed to participate in society according to a "contract."

There are a lot of problems with this picture. Individuals are not isolated and autonomous but are inevitably products of and participants in society. Furthermore, few individuals can be said to have genuinely agreed to their place in society—as if there is any real alternative!

Another problem with the focus on privacy is that privacy means different things to different people and means different things in different cultures. (Even so, there may be commonalities in attitudes to privacy across the most divergent cultures.[4]) But people who have different concepts of privacy may agree to oppose particular types of surveillance.

A focus on privacy directs attention to the individual whose privacy is invaded; a focus on surveillance directs attention to the exercise of power and to the groups that undertake it. Whether antisurveillance is a better rallying point than privacy, though, remains to be seen.

---

[4] Barrington Moore, Jr., *Privacy: Studies in Social and Cultural History* (Armonk, NY: M. E. Sharpe, 1984).

Reform solutions

One way proposed to protect privacy is to ensure that all the people who have access to information collected about members of the public deal with it in a "responsible" fashion. This means that those who deal with or have responsibility for information—such as computer administrators, police, government bureaucrats, telephone technicians and personnel managers—should have the highest personal standards. For example, they should use the information only for the purposes for which it was collected. Codes of ethics are sometimes proposed to set a standard of behaviour.

Most bank managers, marketeers, hospital administrators, government officials and the like are responsible people who are unlikely to misuse the information at their disposal. But all it takes is a minority of less responsible people for serious breaches of confidentiality to occur.

However, even if every single person with access to confidential data was absolutely trustworthy, this would not solve the problem. This is because there are enormous bureaucratic pressures to extend the use of data about individuals for, from the organisation's point of view, very sound reasons. The tax office wants to collect data to ensure that all pay their fair share of tax, so that enough money is available for essential public spending. Government bureaucracies keep data on welfare recipients in order to make sure that only those who really need benefits actually receive them; with limited funds, making payments to those who don't need them means less for those who do. Marketeers collect information on consumers in order to increase their profits, to be sure, but they sincerely believe they are aiming to provide a better service or product to those who really need it. Police see surveillance as necessary to protect the community from serious crime.

One may argue that these attitudes are rationalisations for policies that benefit those defending the surveillance, namely the salaries of government bureaucrats, etc. But it would be unfair to accuse people of bad intentions. It is only a tiny minority of snoopers who gather information for the purpose of blackmail. Almost all surveillance is carried out by well-meaning people with what they believe are the most worthy ends in mind.

Furthermore, there is a lot of public support for surveillance to stop cheats and crooks. Bureaucratic and popular pressures often reinforce each other, egged on by media stories of welfare abuse or dangerous criminals.

When a government department proposes to compare tax records with lists of recipients of unemployment benefits, a central motivation is to save money by exposing those on good salaries who are also improperly obtaining unemployment payments. What could be more sensible, indeed laudable? Ensuring that everyone in the system is highly responsible will eliminate some of the abuses but will not address the bureaucratic and commercial pressures for ever greater collection and combination of data about individuals. In summary, codes of ethics and other methods to ensure responsible use of information are all very well but don't address institutional pressures to expand surveillance.

Another way of opposing surveillance is for governments to pass laws and establish agencies and systems to protect privacy. Many writers on privacy favour this approach. Laws, regulations and privacy commissions can, indeed, accomplish many things. They can allow citizens to see and correct files held on them; they can outlaw certain practices, such as sharing of databases; they can ensure that privacy considerations become a factor in policy making; they can establish organisations that keep tabs on technical developments; they can impose penalties on violators of people's privacy.

This sounds well and good. The people who propose and implement these solutions are undoubtedly well-intentioned. But the whole approach is fundamentally flawed.

One big problem is that the path of legal regulation assumes a trade-off between privacy and other benefits, such as profit or bureaucratic efficiency. In the balance, privacy usually comes off second best. There are clear and direct advantages to corporations and government departments in expanding their capacities to gather and manipulate information on citizens. By contrast, there are few powerful groups with any direct interest in protecting the privacy of the "ordinary citizen." The result is that privacy concerns are routinely squashed by the steamroller of surveillance.

It is risky to rely mainly on governments to provide protection against surveillance when governments themselves are responsible for much of it. The very existence of the government depends on collecting taxes. So when government needs for tax money meet citizen resistance to further impositions, it becomes difficult to argue against extra measures to stop "tax cheats," even when these measures involve accumulating ever more information about individuals. The state also depends for its existence on the police, military and spy agencies to detect and thwart external and internal challenges. These arms of the state are well known to thrive on information collected through surveillance.

In practice, the main role of laws protecting privacy may be to give the illusion that the problem is being dealt with. Certainly that is the case for the Privacy Commission in Australia, whose task is to make recommendations on how to maintain privacy within the present laws. The Commission can do nothing to challenge existing laws. So when the Australian government decided to allow tax records and other records to be combined—something it had earlier promised not to do—the Privacy Commission could only sit there and make recommendations within the framework of the new policy.[5]

It is unrealistic to expect governments to take the lead in countering the driving forces behind increasing surveillance. True, the state is not a unified entity, so there can be groups inside pushing against as well as for surveillance. But as long as

---

[5] Davies (see note 1), chapter 6, "Why the watchdog never barks."

the state depends fundamentally on maintaining power over citizens—and it must, in order to extract resources to support itself and to defend itself against internal and external enemies— the state cannot be a reliable ally against surveillance, since surveillance grows out of and supports the power of the state.

The power to undertake surveillance and use the information obtained is corrupting. That explains why reform solutions are inadequate.

Technical solutions

Another way to deal with problems of surveillance is to implement technical fixes. An example is public key encryption for electronic communications.

Consider a person who uses a computer to generate a message that is communicated through the telephone network to another computer. Surveillance of this message is possible by tapping into the network and deciphering the computer text. Now add encryption: the sender uses a little program to turn their message into code, using their own private key and the receiver's public key. The receiver is able to decipher the message by using the receiver's private key and the sender's public key. The receiver also knows that the message could only have come from the sender, for whom the key thus is an electronic signature. This can be done using ordinary desktop computers using freely available software.

Naturally, spy agencies do not like it. The United States National Security Agency has pushed for keys designed by the NSA itself. Others suspect that the NSA will design the key so that it can break the code and be able to read all telecommunications. Individual users, by contrast, want a system to guarantee the integrity of their messages.[6]

Many government and corporate elites won't be attracted to public key encryption either. They prefer encryption systems

---

[6] Lance J. Hoffman (ed.), *Building in Big Brother: The Cryptographic Policy Debate* (New York: Springer-Verlag, 1995).

which ensure that they can find out what their employees or clients are communicating.

One lesson from this debate is that technical solutions are not automatically implemented, however logical they may appear. Technical approaches to collecting and processing information are the product of the exercise of power. In the case of public key encryption, the power struggle is visible. Usually such struggles are not.

Technical choices pervade privacy issues. They are involved in designing questionnaires and standard forms. (Why, for example, should I have to provide my social security number when assigning copyright of an article to a publisher?). They are involved in setting up computer databases. They are involved in establishing standards for telecommunication systems. These and other technical choices involve the exercise of power. A technical fix is not an easy solution to the problem of surveillance, but simply another arena for the same basic debates.

Disrupting surveillance

Surprising as it may seem, much surveillance depends on cooperation or acquiescence by the person about whom information is collected, such as when we fill out forms. As well, the cooperation or acquiescence of various workers is required for surveillance to be successful. These dependencies suggest a number of measures to corrupt databases. I will comment afterwards on the disadvantages of this approach.

• Disrupters can fill out forms with small mistakes in their names, addresses, and other details. This will create multiple entries in databases and make it more difficult for database matches to be successful.

• Disrupters can fill out forms with imaginary information, or with information about famous people (or about database managers). This will swamp the database with incorrect information.

• Workers who key in data from forms can introduce mistakes.

- Computer programmers can corrupt files. A subtle approach is to make changes that reduce the value of files, for example replacing the occasional number "0" by "1" or replacing the occasional letter "a" by "e." (Just imagine how this would affect a record of personal data about yourself.)
- Computer programmers can take more drastic action against files, for example totally erasing databases (and backup copies). There are a number of destructive techniques, such as logic bombs, Trojan horses and computer viruses.
- One needn't be a computer specialist to be disruptive. A magnet can be quite sufficient to damage computer tapes and discs, and pulling out a few circuit boards can disable a computer.
- In the face of direct surveillance by bugs or observation, a range of devious techniques can be imagined, such as disguises and misleading taped messages.

These sorts of antisurveillance tactics are in the great tradition of the Luddites, the British workers of the early 1800s who are remembered for smashing the machines that put them out of work but who had a much more developed political programme than is usually recognised. In assessing the disruption programme for antisurveillance, it is worthwhile to mention some contemporary sabotage activities. A considerable amount of workplace sabotage occurs, almost entirely on an individual basis.[7] There is little in the way of an organised movement to use such disruptive tactics. There is, though, some advocacy. The magazine *Processed World* has given sympathetic treatment to office workers who subvert business-as-usual through workplace sabotage. David Noble has written the most sophisticated argument for such techniques as a way for workers to challenge the power of management and capitalism.[8]

---

[7] Martin Sprouse with Lydia Ely (ed.), *Sabotage in the American Workplace* (San Francisco: Pressure Drop Press, 1992).

[8] David F. Noble, *Progress Without People: In Defense of Luddism* (Chicago: Charles H. Kerr, 1993).

Methods of sabotage have been adopted openly by radical environmentalists under the banner of Earth First!, with the goal of protecting wilderness from governments and corporations. Their practical manuals describe techniques for pulling out survey stakes, defacing billboards, spiking trees and incapacitating bulldozers, among others. They advocate only those techniques that avoid any risk of injury to others. Their first priority is not to be caught. It should be noted that Earth First!ers also use a range of open and nondestructive methods, such as rallies and sitting in trees.[9]

Corrupting databases and other ways of disrupting surveillance challenge the encroachments of the surveillance society, but they have a number of limitations. Introducing errors into databases sounds effective, but databases are full of errors already. How much difference would more errors make? The impact would need to be financially significant (even more wrong names on mailing lists!) or politically potent (names of powerful people on embarrassing lists).

More importantly, disrupting surveillance in this fashion is, by necessity, mostly an individual activity. It provides a poor basis for mobilising a social movement; instead, it tends to breed secrecy and vanguards. Such secret activities are ideal for the duels of spy versus counterspy. When it comes to spying and infiltration, social movements are likely to come off second best to state agencies.

This was certainly the case with Earth First!, which was infiltrated by the FBI. Some Earth First!ers have renounced sabotage and secret tactics and, as a result, been able to forge links with workers in a way impossible using individualist, secretive methods.

Instead of disrupting the surveillance that is carried out *by* powerful organisations, another approach is to undertake "countersurveillance": surveillance *of* powerful organisations.

[9] Dave Foreman and Bill Haywood (eds.), *Ecodefense: A Field Guide to Monkeywrenching* (Tucson, AZ: Ned Ludd Books, 1988, 2nd edition); *Earth First! Direct Action Manual* (Eugene, OR: DAM Collective, 1997).

Today, large organisations and powerful individuals have as much privacy as money will buy, and most surveillance is carried out against the weak, disorganised and defenceless. The builders of weapons of mass destruction use every available means to ensure secrecy while spying on their enemies (foreign powers and peace movements). Can this pattern be challenged and reversed by promoting surveillance of the rich, powerful and dangerous?

The challenge is enormous, but some courageous individuals and groups have made efforts in this direction. A few investigators have probed the corridors of power.[10] Their exposés are incredibly threatening to organisational elites simply because they reveal what is actually happening on the inside. Such information undoubtedly contributes to better strategies by social movements. Many more exposés are needed. Even more daring is spying on spies and publicising the results, such as the efforts of the magazine *Counterspy* to expose CIA agents. This was so threatening to the spy agency that special legislation was passed to stop such revelations.

Much more could be said of the potential for disrupting surveillance. The techniques to do this deserve much more study and experimentation. It does seem, though, that they offer at most one part of a solution: they interfere with surveillance but do not offer an alternative to the systems that generate and thrive on it. Furthermore, as the experience of Earth First! has shown, disruption sometimes triggers increased surveillance and repression. To achieve a society with less surveillance, disruption is far from an ideal approach.

Institutional change

Here I outline some radical approaches to eliminating surveillance by eliminating the institutional capacity or need for it in

---

[10] See for example articles in *CovertAction Quarterly* and Nicky Hager, *Secret Power: New Zealand's Role in the International Spy Network* (Nelson, New Zealand: Craig Potton, 1996).

the first place. By necessity, this is an extremely brief overview, but it should illustrate the general approach.

Many of the proposals here, such as "abolish nuclear weapons" or "abolish the state," are easy to say but very difficult to accomplish. After all, it's a challenging, long-term process to succeed in abolishing nuclear weapons, not to mention abolishing the state. It is not my intention to present strategies for achieving these goals; in most cases, there are well-established perspectives or movements for doing so. Rather, my intention is to point out institutional sources of surveillance so that campaigns against surveillance can be chosen and implemented in ways that weaken rather than strengthen them.

To put this another way: abolishing nuclear weapons or the state is not a prerequisite for eliminating surveillance. Rather, campaigns against nuclear weapons or the state should be developed so that they are compatible with struggles against surveillance, and campaigns against surveillance should be developed so that they are compatible with struggles with the ultimate aim of abolishing nuclear weapons, abolishing the state or eliminating other roots of surveillance. In short, a programme for institutional change provides a *direction* for antisurveillance campaigns today.

Dangerous technologies

Surveillance has been justified by the need to protect against the dangers of technologies. Given the existence of the technologies, surveillance makes a lot of sense. One way to eliminate the surveillance is to eliminate the technologies.

Military spying is needed to protect against unauthorised access to nuclear and other weapons. The solution is to abolish these weapons.

Nuclear power is potentially dangerous. Hazards include reactor accidents, terrorist use of nuclear materials and proliferation of nuclear weapons capabilities through "civilian" nuclear programmes. Nuclear power therefore brings with it the necessity for surveillance. There have been special police forces for nuclear facilities, as well as spying on anti-nuclear power groups. One of the earliest objections to nuclear power was the tendencies towards a police state inherent in a nuclear society.[11] The solution is straightforward: abolish nuclear power. (Eliminating nuclear weapons and nuclear power would still leave the problem of nuclear waste, for which "surveillance" would be required. But surveillance of waste is a different matter from surveillance of individuals, not raising quite the same issues of power inequality.)

A more commonplace dangerous technology is the car. The danger of traffic accidents has engendered a multitude of traffic regulations and the attentions of police. There are laws requiring wearing of seat belts and laws prohibiting high blood alcohol levels. The automobilised society thus brings with it considerable invasions of personal privacy. Cameras already watch over dangerous intersections. As well, there is increasing use of systems for automatic electronic identification of road vehicles, in order to reduce congestion or charge for road use, or both. A computer can record when your car passes a monitor underneath or beside the road.

Far from cars enjoying "freedom of the road," they actually do more to put people on police files than any other technology today. The solution is to move towards a society in which cars play a much smaller role. Proper town planning, which makes it easy for people to live affordably near workplace, shops and amenities, can greatly reduce the need for cars, and make walking and cycling much more attractive. For longer distances, cheap public transport offers a service without the rationale that surveillance is needed to avoid accidents.

Medical records

Records of a patient's medical treatment can, in the wrong hands, be used to embarrass or discriminate against them. Hospital personnel are known to "browse" through computer

---

[11] Robert Jungt, *The New Tyranny* (New York: Grosset & Dunlap, 1979).

records on patients, just to pass the time or to look for people whose names they recognise. Hospitals sometimes make special efforts to ensure the privacy of prominent individuals, protecting their records from routine observation.

The simple solution is for patients to keep their own medical files. They could, if desired, give copies to anyone they trusted, whether a family member, a friend, their doctor or indeed a hospital.

Prisons

Prisons are the ultimate in surveillance. The prisoner is both constrained and observed. There are several ways to reduce the number of prisoners and hence the extent of surveillance. One is to abolish victimless crimes, such as for vagrancy and drug use. Another is to increase social equity, so that there is less incentive for crime.

The ultimate aim should be to abolish prisons. After all, they do not reduce the crime rate and are an insult to human dignity. Prisons should be replaced by a range of methods and policies genuinely oriented towards rehabilitation.[12]

Workplaces

Workers are monitored on the job by management to maintain output but also to keep workers under control. The alternative is for workers to control their own work collectively.

This alternative includes semi-autonomous work groups, in which workers decide the way they will do a job within the general framework set down by management. It includes collectives, in which all workers as a group make the crucial decisions about what to produce and how to carry out their jobs. It includes workers' control—usually associated with larger organisations—in which workers make the basic decisions about their enterprise and work, using decision-making methods including voting, delegate systems, and rotation through managerial

---

[12] Thomas Mathiesen, *Prison on Trial: A Critical Assessment* (London: Sage, 1990).

positions. In addition, methods of production can be selected or changed to facilitate workers' control.[13]

It should be noted that under workers' self-management, what a worker does is still watched by others. The difference is that it is workmates who do the watching, not managers. This is a change in the distribution of power. Self-management should be distinguished from techniques such as Total Quality Management, which also involve workers watching each other, but in a system designed by management to extract the greatest profit while maintaining managerial control.

Spy agencies

Organisations such as the FBI, MI5 and KGB, which are found in countries throughout the world, are responsible for some of the most objectionable snooping. They escape serious scrutiny by claiming the higher needs of "national security."[14]

There is a simple solution to surveillance by spy agencies: the agencies should be abolished. These organisations mainly serve their own ends and the ends of state elites. The chief targets of spy agencies are not foreign spies but domestic citizens. There has never been an open and honest assessment of their value to the wider community. Such assessments are prevented by secrecy provisions.

What about preventing terrorism? Spy agencies have probably done more to promote than to prevent terrorism, especially remembering that most terrorism is carried out by governments. A grassroots antiterrorism programme would include serious attention to the grievances of minority groups (whose members may resort to terrorism to gain a hearing) and community-level communication and solidarity.

---

[13] Gerry Hunnius, G. David Garson and John Case (eds.), *Workers' Control: A Reader on Labor and Social Change* (New York: Vintage, 1973); Paul Mattick, *Anti-Bolshevik Communism* (London: Merlin, 1978); Ernie Roberts, *Workers' Control* (London: Allen and Unwin, 1973).

[14] A revealing account of the use of private investigators by British spy agencies is Gary Murray, *Enemies of the State* (London: Simon & Schuster, 1993).

What about defence secrets? These should be made obsolete by abolishing the military and replacing it with community-based methods of nonviolent defence, which require little or no secrecy.[15]

Government services

Information is collected by governments to make sure that recipients of services are genuine. This applies to unemployment benefits, child support schemes, pensions for people with disabilities, war veteran benefits, education support schemes, health benefits, and the like. Keeping detailed information on recipients is considered essential to prevent cheating, in order to keep costs down.

One solution is to provide basic services free to anyone who wants them. This applies today to services such as public parks and public libraries. Why not also to food, shelter and health services? The basic principle is that services for identified individuals are replaced by collective provision, for which there is no need for individuals to be identified.

To address the ramifications of such changes would be an enormous task. Let me outline a few cases. Consider food. Basic staples could be provided at community centres to anyone who wanted them (possibly with donations invited to help cover costs). This would be quite possible with today's production, which is more than ample to feed everyone if distributed appropriately (including in most of the countries where people die of starvation).[16] In many countries, governments control markets in order to limit production. Such schemes would become unnecessary.

Consider health services. The escalation of costs here comes primarily from intensive interventions using expensive technology. Most of the services that make a big difference to people's

---

[15] Brian Martin, *Social Defence, Social Change* (London: Freedom Press, 1993).

[16] Susan George, *How the Other Half Dies: The Real Reasons for World Hunger* (Montclair, NJ: Allanheld, Osmun, 1977); Frances Moore Lappé and Joseph Collins with Cary Fowler, *Food First: Beyond the Myth of Scarcity* (Boston: Houghton Mifflin, 1977).

health don't have to cost a lot. Generic drugs could be provided free or at nominal cost. Many more people could be trained to administer basic health care. Emphasis could be shifted from curative methods to prevention by improving diet, exercise and occupational health and safety.

Private investigative agencies

Private agencies undertake a significant amount of surveillance, but it is small in volume compared to listening operations and databases by governments and large corporations. But the private agencies usually are collecting information about a particular individual, and so their actions tend to be especially objectionable.

A large fraction of private spying is for the purpose of bolstering a disputed claim. For example, an insurance company may hire a company to watch a person who has claimed to have received a back injury at work. Films of the person playing golf or putting out the wash can then be produced in court to undermine the compensation claim.

The incentive for this sort of spying comes from fault-based compensation systems: if the employer is responsible, then there's a big pay-out to the worker. Fault-based systems are common in areas such as military veterans' benefits, divorce proceedings and automobile accidents as well as workers' health. The solution here is to eliminate fault-based compensation systems. No-fault systems of comprehensive insurance overcome the inequities of fault-based systems and have been shown to greatly reduce costs.

Commercial databases

Companies collect an enormous amount of information on potential consumers, which they use to help design products and marketing strategies. Banks and credit agencies collect information on credit worthiness. A future cashless society with widespread use of electronic funds transfer for purchases would leave an electronic record of consumer behaviour unprecedented in detail.

Large corporations in a market will inevitably become involved in mass marketing. The availability of cheap and powerful computing capabilities means that the extensive use of databases is impossible to control in this situation. There are two institutional revolutions that would undercut the drive for consumer surveillance: abolishing large corporations and abolishing the market, or both.

Abolishing large corporations but retaining markets is a vision of many libertarians and free-market anarchists. (Also essential for their project is reduction of the state to a minimal set of functions.) In an economy in which large bureaucratic organisations are not viable, entrepreneurs would mainly trade in local or specialist markets. An individual entrepreneur would undoubtedly collect information about potential buyers and sellers. But the potential dangers of large databases would be minimised, because the various buyers and sellers in the market would have similar, limited degrees of power. The unequal relationship of the large, powerful corporation with respect to the individual consumer would be eliminated.

An alternative way to undermine commercial surveillance of consumers is to abolish the market and replace it by local self-management by workers and community members. (In this vision, the state is totally eliminated.) This is the project of anarchists or, in other words, libertarian socialists. In this model, the production and distribution of goods and services is done on a cooperative basis, rather than the competitive principles built into the market. Various cooperative enterprises would undertake tasks of necessity to the community, deciding for themselves, in consultation with other enterprises and organisations, priorities and methods.[17]

In such a system, there would be no incentive to collect information about large numbers of isolated consumers, since

---

[17] See, for example, Jenny Thornley, *Workers' Co-operatives: Jobs and Dreams* (London: Heinemann, 1981).

marketing in the capitalist sense would not exist. More importantly, power relationships would be much more equal, so that the foundation for surveillance would not be present.

Taxation

Governments are built on taxation. Without taxation—or, more generally, the extraction of resources from the economy—the state could not exist. In earlier eras, governments could survive using only excise duties and taxation of large estates. But as the modern state expanded in size and power with the triumph of capitalism over feudalism, the demand for more and more information about individual citizens also expanded. This is not just to collect taxes but also to distribute government services, which help justify the state.

Computers have added extra technological capabilities to the state's thirst for information, but the thirst was there long before computers. The rise of the modern state was a process of central bureaucracies entering communities, collecting information, assessing taxes and conscripting soldiers.[18]

Since surveillance is central to the existence of the state, reform is hardly enough. The radical solution is to abolish the state. The alternative is communities organised around self-management, as outlined above.[19]

From vision to strategy

This institutional change programme is radical, going to the roots of the problem of surveillance. It is hardly a practical proposition, though, to implement these solutions through a short, sharp campaign. What use, then, is the programme?

---

[18] Henry Jacoby, *The Bureaucratization of the World* (Berkeley: University of California Press, 1973); Charles Tilly (ed.), *The Formation of National States in Western Europe* (Princeton: Princeton University Press, 1975).

[19] See, for example, Michael Bakunin, *Bakunin on Anarchy* (edited by Sam Dolgoff) (New York: Vintage, 1971); Daniel Guérin, *Anarchy: From Theory to Practice* (New York: Monthly Review Press, 1970); Colin Ward, *Anarchy in Action* (London: Freedom Press, 1982).

First, it draws attention to the way that surveillance is deeply embedded in today's social institutions and is becoming more and more pervasive. The real idealism is to imagine that the problem can be solved by legislative and regulatory measures by the very institutions that are responsible for the problem. The radical agenda should warn against investing too much energy or hope in reform efforts, which may give only an illusion of protection.

Second, the programme provides an *additional* argument to challenge and replace hierarchical social structures. Alone, the problem of surveillance is hardly serious enough to question the value of nuclear power, corporate capitalism or the state. But surveillance is an important factor which should not be neglected in a focus on environmental impacts, war or exploitation of workers.

Third, the programme highlights the range of triggers for surveillance: "national security," marketing, protection against dangerous technologies, provision of welfare. There is no evil agency that is responsible for all surveillance.

Undoubtedly, most surveillance is carried out with the very best of intentions: to protect the nation, to provide better products to consumers, to economise on government expenditure. Surveillance is not a product of evil schemers. The debate over surveillance concerns different conceptions of the good.

Fourth, a programme of radical solutions provides a *direction* for campaigns today. While it is impossible to introduce collective provision or to abolish the state overnight, it is quite sensible to examine campaigns to see whether they aid the capacity for community self-reliance and whether they weaken rather than strengthen the power of the state.

5

Free speech versus bureaucracy

Bureaucratic elites control information in order to help maintain their control. When employees speak out, this is a challenge to bureaucratic power and its corruptions.

Bureaucracy is a way of organising work. It involves hierarchy, in which people at higher levels are bosses of those below, and so on down the chain. It also involves the division of labour, in which some people do one thing and others do other things—cleaners, accountants, researchers, managers, etc. Other characteristic features of bureaucracy are rules which describe the duties of members, standard operating procedures and impersonal relations between members. Not every bureaucracy has all these characteristics. The most important features are hierarchy and division of labour. Another way of thinking about bureaucracy is as a way of organising work in which people are treated as interchangeable and replaceable cogs to fill specialised roles.

The word "bureaucracy" is popularly applied to government bodies, such as the taxation office and welfare agencies. Any sort of organisation can potentially be a bureaucracy: a corporation, a church, a trade union, an army, a political party, an

environmental group. In fact, most large organisations in the
world today are organised bureaucratically.[1]

There are a number of consequences of bureaucracy. Since
control is exercised from the top, many at the bottom have a low
commitment to work. Since knowledge can be used to exercise
power, top bureaucrats are reluctant to reveal information to
outsiders or to lower level workers. Since top positions in
bureaucracies give power and privilege, preserving the bureaucratic structure can become a higher priority than accomplishing
what the bureaucracy was set up for. Since bosses exercise
control by insisting on following standard operating procedures,
doing a job according to standard procedures can become more
important than doing the job well.

Bureaucracy only became the main way of organising work
in the past couple of centuries. It's worth recalling some non-
bureaucratic ways of organising work:

- individual initiative
- family
- feudal estates
- free market
- self-managing collectives
- automation.

From this list, it should be apparent that bureaucracies have both
advantages and disadvantages, depending on what the alternative is. An individual can work alone without bothering about
hierarchy or division of labour, but there's a limit to what one
person can do alone. Families can do more, but not everyone is

---

[1] Bengt Abrahamsson, *Bureaucracy or Participation: The Logic of Organization*
(Beverly Hills, CA: Sage, 1977); Ralph P. Hummel, *The Bureaucratic Experience*
(New York: St. Martin's Press, 1977); Henry Jacoby, *The Bureaucratization of the
World* (Berkeley: University of California Press, 1973); Katherine Newman,
'Incipient bureaucracy: the development of hierarchy in egalitarian organizations',
in Gerald M. Britan and Ronald Cohen (eds.), *Hierarchy and Society:
Anthropological Perspectives on Bureaucracy* (Philadelphia: Institute for the Study
of Human Issues, 1980), pp. 143-164; Charles Perrow, *Complex Organizations: A
Critical Essay* (Glenview, IL: Scott, Foresman and Company, 1979).

happy with their position in a family. One of the great advantages of bureaucracy is that it promises to overcome the nepotism and favouritism that is common in enterprises dominated by family connections, which usually means dominated by a patriarch. In a bureaucracy, appointments and promotions are supposed to be decided on merit, not who your father is or where you went to school. That is a great attraction compared to feudal systems. Of course, few bureaucracies completely measure up to their promise of fair treatment.

Because bureaucracy is a system of power, it has a strong tendency to mesh with other systems of power—such as male domination. Most bureaucratic elites are men. Men get into top positions in bureaucracies and use their power to exclude women. This can be by blatant discrimination, subtle harassment or by fostering expectations of the style of a successful bureaucrat, which tend to be masculine characteristics. Male domination in a bureaucracy is then used to get other men to support the bureaucratic hierarchy. Bureaucracy and patriarchy thus engage in a process of "mutual mobilisation."

The same process can work with other systems of power. Bureaucratic elites can be linked to:
- family members;
- religious groups;
- ethnic groups;
- ideological stands;
- people from a particular background, such as certain schools, usually from the same social class;
- personal networks of patronage, based on giving and receiving favours.

Thus, although bureaucracy is supposed to be based on merit, it is commonly "corrupted" by other systems of power. Rather than being an exceptional deviation from the norm, such corruptions are to be expected in any system based on highly unequal power. The result is that most bureaucracies seethe with rumours, power plays, upheavals, takeovers and changing organisational structures.[2] This reality is covered over by the rhetoric of efficiency, merit, competition, customer orientation or whatever is the latest buzz word.

Information and bureaucratic power

Information is a crucial part of any bureaucratic system. Normally, information about operations is passed up the hierarchy and orders from bosses are passed down. In practice, neither process operates according to the ideal. Because workers are afraid of the consequences of telling the truth, they commonly tell bosses what they think the bosses want to hear. The top managers thus can become quite out of touch with what's happening. Similarly, when orders are passed down the chain, they may be ignored, reinterpreted or manipulated, in many cases just so workers can get on with the job.

Bureaucratic elites like to collect information about workers, from personal details to comments on job performance. This information can be used to control the workers. On the other hand, information about the elites is not made available to workers. In other words, surveillance is natural to bureaucracies, and much of it is targeted at workers.

Bureaucratic elites have considerable power and, as usual, it tends to corrupt. When possible, elites give themselves high salaries, plush offices, grandiose titles and special privileges. They can exercise power by supporting workers who support them personally and by penalising those who criticise or just annoy them. They can foster fear by intimidating subordinates. They can create havoc through reprimands, demotions, dismissals, restructuring and a host of other mechanisms. Just about anyone who has worked in a bureaucracy has a good idea of the sort of problems that can arise.

---

2 Robert Jackall, *Moral Mazes: The World of Corporate Managers* (New York: Oxford University Press, 1988), describes this process with great insight.

A bureaucracy is not a free society. There are no elections for top offices. There is little free speech, and there is no free press for opponents of the current elites. Open opponents of the ruling group are likely to be harassed, demoted or dismissed. There is no independent judiciary to deal with grievances.

In fact, a bureaucracy is rather similar to an authoritarian state.[3] The most important difference is that an authoritarian state can use the army and police against internal opponents. Bureaucratic elites normally can use only methods such as demotion and dismissal—there are no formal systems to use violence. (In a few bureaucracies, such as the army, force can be used officially against dissident employees.) These methods are potent enough for many purposes.

Bureaucratic elites also control information in order to maintain power in relation to other organisations. If a corporation reveals its plans to competitors, it is vulnerable to challenge or even takeover. If a government department reveals its internal operations, it makes itself vulnerable to critics, whether politicians, other government departments or lobby groups.

Finally, bureaucratic elites control information to cover up corruption and bad or dangerous decisions. Tobacco companies covered up research showing the addictiveness of cigarettes. Police cover up bribery and incompetence. Politicians pass laws to prevent release of government documents dealing with "national security" in order to cover up embarrassing actions.

Free speech by employees is a potent threat to bureaucratic elites. It threatens to undermine elite control in the bureaucracy itself, it threatens to weaken bureaucratic elites in relation to other organisations, and it threatens to expose dubious decisions and corrupt practices by the elites themselves. It is precisely for these reasons that free speech for employees is vital as both a method and a goal.

---

[3] Deena Weinstein, *Bureaucratic Opposition: Challenging Abuses at the Workplace* (New York: Pergamon, 1979).

Arguments

Various arguments are put forward to justify the controls imposed on speech by employees. It's worth examining a few of these.[4]

- *Employees get paid. They shouldn't expect anything else.* Why not? In other circumstances—outside of bureaucracies—payment is not allowed as an excuse to deny people freedom of speech. Shareholders receive dividends. Do they lose their right to speak out?

- *Free speech will reveal trade secrets.* Perhaps so, but this isn't such a big deal. Corporations spend large amounts of money on industrial espionage, including hiring staff from other companies as well as covert listening. Free speech would make this process more honest and open.

  Anyway, society benefits when good ideas are widely known. Corporate innovation can be improved when ideas "leak" out.[5] Overall, secrecy is not an advantage, even for corporations.

  Industrial societies have the capacity to produce plenty of goods for everyone. Overproduction is a far greater problem than underproduction. Therefore, one of the most important aims of work should be to provide a satisfying experience for the workers.

- *Employees agree to keep quiet as part of their voluntarily accepted employment contract.* The so-called employment contract is quite one-sided. Few workers have easy mobility. They don't have the financial resources available to employers.

---

4 Many of these points are taken from David W. Ewing, *Freedom Inside the Organization: Bringing Civil Liberties to the Workplace* (New York: E. P. Dutton, 1977), a nice treatment of the case for employee rights.

5 Stuart Macdonald, "Nothing either good or bad: industrial espionage and technology transfer," *International Journal of Technology Management,* Vol. 8, Nos. 1/2, 1993, pp. 95-105.

- *Employers have a right to run their enterprises the way they want.* Certainly not. The "rights" of employers are restricted in lots of ways. Laws prevent hiring of some people, such as children; laws prevent hazardous working conditions; laws prevent indiscriminate impacts on the environment. Enterprises are part of society, and impacts on the society are taken seriously—including impacts on stockholders, clients and other enterprises.

When there is control over speech, those who decide on and exercise the control have power over others. This power is corrupting. It can be used to cover up abuses by elites and to attack those who might challenge the elites. This is precisely how it is used in practice.

Most people believe that "good speech"—speech that is informed and enlightened—should be encouraged. Elites argue that they must control the "bad speech" of others so that only "good speech" is allowed, namely only things that have their approval. But there is a different way to challenge "bad speech"—by challenging it with dialogue and debate. Only by encouraging people's capacity for critical thinking and argumentation will "good speech" become the genuine voice of the people.

Whistleblowing[6]

Generally speaking, whistleblowing is an act of dissent. Researcher Bill De Maria gives the following more specific definition. Whistleblowing is:

— an open disclosure about significant wrongdoing
— made by a concerned citizen totally or predominantly motivated by notions of public interest,

---

[6] One excellent treatment is Myron Peretz Glazer and Penina Migdal Glazer, *The Whistleblowers: Exposing Corruption in Government and Industry* (New York: Basic Books, 1989). For more information, see
http://www.uow.edu.au/arts/sts/bmartin/dissent/.

— who has perceived the wrongdoing in a particular role
— who initiates the disclosure of her or his own free will
— to a person or agency capable of investigating the complaint and facilitating the correction of wrongdoing.[7]

In this narrow sense, whistleblowers are usually government or corporate employees who speak out to expose corruption or dangers to the public or environment. Whistleblowers thus practise free speech as a method of exposing problems that they perceive in their workplace. This seems to be a good thing: what could be more worthy than pointing out corruption or hazards so that they can be dealt with?

The problem is that whistleblowing is commonly a threat to powerful interests, typically the employee's superiors. Rather than rectifying the problem, it is common for whistleblowers to come under attack. They are threatened, ostracised, harassed, transferred, reprimanded, vilified, referred to psychiatrists, demoted, dismissed and blacklisted.

David Obendorf was a veterinary pathologist who worked in Launceston, Tasmania for the state's Department of Primary Industry and Fisheries (DPIF). He became concerned about government cutbacks to disease surveillance services, which he believed were important for preventing outbreaks of disease among stock in local farms. His public statements were not welcomed by his superiors. He was transferred across the state to Hobart into a policy position for which he was not trained or suited. Then he was transferred back to Launceston into an office with no computer, no light fitting and broken castors on the chair. More seriously, the information was spread around the locality that he was gay (true), that his partner had died of AIDS (true), that he had AIDS (false) and that his statements were a product of "AIDS dementia" (false). The rumour-mongering undermined his credibility in the conservative rural area in which he worked.

---

[7] William De Maria, "Quarantining dissent: the Queensland public sector ethics movement," *Australian Journal of Public Administration,* Vol. 54, No. 4, December 1995, pp. 442-454, at p. 447.

The curious thing about this case is that everything Obendorf said had been acknowledged in DPIF's own documents. The difference was that he was making the points accessible to the public in talks and statements to the media.

For years, rumours had circulated that some Australian diplomats, especially in southeast Asia, regularly had sex with children, but little or no action was taken to investigate or stop the practice. Alastair Gaisford, an employee in the Department of Foreign Affairs and Trade (DFAT) in Canberra, Australia, was one of a small number of DFAT workers who spoke out about paedophilia in the foreign service. In 1996, DFAT officials took disciplinary action against Gaisford. As well, they asked Federal Police to raid Gaisford's home to collect documents.

The government minister in charge of DFAT, Alexander Downer, had made a public statement inviting anyone with information about paedophilia in the department to come forward. But this rhetoric made little impact on DFAT top bureaucrats, who went ahead with their harassment of Gaisford. There was much more initiative taken against DFAT whistle-blowers than to get to the bottom of allegations about paedophilia.

In general terms, whistleblowing can be thought of as the exercise of free speech to challenge injustice. The hope of the whistleblower is that when top officials realise the problem, they will take action to deal with it. What they commonly discover afterwards is that bureaucratic elites are far more concerned about covering up the problem than dealing with it. In all this, information and credibility are crucial elements.

In a tiny minority of cases, whistleblowers are congratulated for pointing out a problem, which is promptly dealt with. I will set these exceptional cases aside in order to concentrate on the typical response: cover up and attack the whistleblower. Authorities will deny that there is any problem. They will refuse to supply documentation. They will undertake reprisals to stop the whistleblower and to deter others.

To have any chance of success, whistleblowers need good documentation. That means that before speaking out, they should collect lots of information, for example copying relevant documents and perhaps getting statements from others. When the crunch comes, authorities often lie. They may deny that documents exist. They may destroy evidence. They sometimes even produce documents that have been altered or totally forged. An important piece of advice for many bureaucratic dissidents is not to speak out immediately, but instead to lie low and collect information, in order to have an irrefutable case.

Whistleblowers typically try formal channels first. They raise their concerns with their immediate boss, the top boss, an internal appeals procedure, an ombudsperson, a member of parliament, a government oversight body, the courts, and any other official body that seems relevant. The most common experience is that formal channels don't work. This seems a sweeping statement. Bill De Maria and Cyrelle Jan collected information from hundreds of whistleblowers who had taken their cases to dozens of different official bodies. Less than one out of ten appeals to an official body gave any sort of positive response.[8]

There is evidence that significant corruption is found in most large police forces. Citizens who complain about corruption usually get nowhere. Police who report corruption by their colleagues can seldom survive in the force. Harassment of police whistleblowers is commonly severe and sometimes brutal.

Why don't the official channels work? At this point it is valuable to remember that bureaucracies are hierarchical. Those higher up are the superiors of those further down. Whistle-blowers expose shortcomings by those higher up than they are. This threatens the hierarchy. Internal appeals procedures are set up by bureaucratic elites and are either staffed by elites or

---

[8] William De Maria and Cyrelle Jan, "Behold the shut-eyed sentry! Whistleblower perspectives on government failure to correct wrongdoing," *Crime, Law & Social Change,* Vol. 24, 1996, pp. 151-166.

employees dependent on them. The result is a strong reluctance to support a person lower down against anyone higher up.

Outside appeal procedures are little better. To take the side of a mere employee against those at the top of an organisation is a frontal challenge to the elites, who are likely to have friends and allies in other organisations. Appeal bodies such as ombudsmen typically have limited funds, limited mandates and little power to bring about change. No wonder they tread softly.

A cynic might suggest that formal procedures and bodies are set up precisely in order to lure dissidents into never-ending appeals, which bog them down in technicalities and trivialities while nothing is done about the problem. Whatever the intent, this is the effect of many procedures and bodies. Information about the problem is kept inside the organisation where it can do little damage.

Whistleblowers usually have far greater impact when they go outside the organisation and official channels, instead taking their message to a wider audience. Media coverage is a particularly potent challenge to a bureaucracy. It takes the issue out of the hands of the bureaucracy and into the eyes of the general public. Top bureaucrats absolutely detest publicity.

Sending a letter to the head of a bureaucracy seldom has much of an impact. Getting the same letter published in a newspaper has a much greater impact. The bureaucrats will all read it, knowing that thousands of others will be reading it too.

Some whistleblower protection laws actually specify that whistleblowers will not be protected if they go to the media. Instead, they have to go to government agencies set up or designated to receive complaints from whistleblowers. This is a good way to keep the problem "in-house." Media coverage allows lots of people to hear about the problem.

It may seem strange recommending media coverage as a benefit to whistleblowers when I have argued that mass media should be replaced with network media. Right now, both bureaucracies and mass media are systems of information inequality and are subject to the corruptions of power. Sometimes one such system can be used against the other, such as when government regulatory bodies restrain large media corporations and when media coverage exposes abuses in bureaucracies. The important thing is not to rely on these sorts of controls, which amount to one powerful group restraining or undermining another. A strategy against corruptions of information power should aim to undermine all these groups.

Sometimes the media will not cover a story, perhaps due to the influence of local vested interests or fear of defamation. The old-fashioned leaflet is one option. Richard Blake, a public servant in New South Wales, helped set up a reform group. The members produced leaflets and on some occasions handed them out to other employees as they entered government buildings. With electronic mail, the potential for distributing information is even greater.

In 1989, David Rindos took up a senior lectureship in the Department of Archaeology at the University of Western Australia. Soon after, he became acting head of the department and was told of serious problems affecting students, including sexual relations between staff and students, favouritism and discrimination. He reported these problems and as a result came under attack himself, eventually being denied tenure in 1993 in spite of more than adequate teaching and research. He pursued his case through the university's formal channels and then tried the Industrial Relations Tribunal, the University Visitor, the Ombudsman and the West Australian Parliament, as well as using Freedom of Information legislation to obtain documents.

The university hierarchy refused to set up a full-scale investigation of the problems originally raised by Rindos and asserted that all proper procedures had been followed in the case of his tenure. In this situation, a lone individual has almost no chance of making any impact on a resolute administration. Rindos and his supporters were able to make progress through publicity. They alerted archaeologists around the world about the tenure denial and subsequently dozens of leading archaeologists wrote to the university in support of Rindos. Media coverage gradually developed. The local *Sunday Times* published many supportive stories. However, the daily *West Australian* published nothing at all until 1996, when it ran a week-long massive attack on Rindos. By this time, though, quite a number of powerful people were convinced that the whole thing needed an independent investigation. Although the university set up its own in-house investigation, the West Australian parliament established a wide-ranging inquiry.

Along the way, Rindos used electronic mail, and occasionally the ordinary post, to powerful effect. He had a mailing list of supporters and interested individuals around the country and beyond. He sent out accounts of the latest events and text of stories in the local media. One of his supporters, Hugh Jarvis in the United States, set up a web site with large numbers of documents about the case. In fact, there was so much material that it became difficult to make sense of the issue at a glance.[9]

Rindos did not gain reinstatement before he died unexpect-edly in 1996 at the age of 49. In addition, he was subject to extremely damaging attacks on his reputation. But he was relatively successful compared to most whistleblowers, who not only suffer harassment and lose their positions but also get bogged down in formal hearings without any real challenge to the things complained about. Rindos achieved a wide degree of recognition about problems with the university and attracted a considerable level of support. As well as using formal channels as methods of redress, he used them as means for generating publicity, for example alerting the media to his submissions, letters of support, documents obtained under FOI, and so forth. He even had a limited success in putting the focus back on the original problems about which he complained rather than on the university's treatment of himself. In December 1997, the

---

[9] See http://www.acsu.buffalo.edu/~hjarvis/rindos.html.

parliamentary committee made its report. It was quite critical of the university.

The goals of bureaucracy

Zygmunt Bauman's *Modernity and the Holocaust* is a stimulating and disturbing book.[10] It is an analysis of the Holocaust— the mass extermination of Jews and other peoples by the Nazis—and how it relates to social institutions in modern society. Bauman believes that the Holocaust has profound implications for our understanding of society, but its study has been relegated to a few specialist areas.

The term "modernity" refers to characteristics of society that have developed only in the past few hundred years, including bureaucracy, rationality, science and, more generally, the separation of ends from means. For example, some scientists work on solving particular puzzles involving reaction rates that are important for modelling the dynamics of nuclear explosions. The scientists work on the way to solve the problem, namely the means. The government and weapons lab administrators decide how to use the research, namely the ends.

Bauman's argument is that bureaucratic rationality was one of the essential factors that made the Holocaust possible. Hitler's goal was to remove the Jews. Various means were tried, such as emigration, but when these failed extermination was the "logical" conclusion, given the premise. The efficient and compliant German bureaucracies carried out the required tasks to reach the "final solution."

The usual explanation of the Holocaust is that it was either a reversion to barbaric behaviour or as something that only related to the Jews. Bauman says, to the contrary, that the Holocaust was made possible by precisely those features of society that made it "civilised." These features remain today.

The "ideal" bureaucracy is highly efficient, with workers

---

[10] Zygmunt Bauman, *Modernity and the Holocaust* (Ithaca: Cornell University Press, 1989).

doing their tasks promptly and reliably. The goals of the bureaucracy are set by others, such as government, owners or top management. The ideal bureaucracy is like a well-functioning piece of equipment. The controller decides how to use it and the machine responds. In the jargon of social science, bureaucracy is a "purposive-rational system."

There are at least two types of bureaucratic whistleblowing.

Procedural whistleblowing

The target here is improper procedures, such as faulty record keeping, neglect of duties, diversion of resources for private purposes, false claims, misuse of money, favouritism, stealing, bullying, blackmail and the like. Some workers are not doing their jobs properly or are actively subverting the aims of the organisation. Procedural whistleblowing exposes the problem that the bureaucracy is not working like it is supposed to, that it falls short of the purposive-rational ideal.

Goal-related whistleblowing

The charge in this case is that the organisation's goals or purposes are inappropriate. For example, a pharmaceutical company could be challenged because it puts the pursuit of profit above public safety, even though it obeys all laws and regulations. Many bureaucracies seek their own survival above all else, even at the expense of their original goals. Goal-related whistleblowing can challenge bureaucratic elites to pursue the original, formal stated goals of the organisation, or to pursue different, better goals.

Both of these sorts of whistleblowing are important, and often they are combined. The message from Bauman is that challenges to procedural shortcomings are not enough, and even bad, if the goals are wrong. The German bureaucracies mounted a programme of exploitation and extermination that was far more deadly than any of the spontaneous anti-Semitism that preceded it. Jews were identified, categorised, sent to work and death camps. Detailed records were kept of ancestry, belongings, labour output and so forth.

It is possible to imagine procedural whistleblowers in Nazi Germany who pointed out that some categories of Jews were being given special treatment, that goods produced by slave labour camps were being diverted for private use, or that there were scams associated with purchase of chemicals used in the gas chambers. Procedural whistleblowers might expose those who protected Jews, such as Oscar Schindler. Since there was massive corruption in Nazi Germany, no doubt such whistle-blowers existed.

By contrast, goal-related whistleblowers would have challenged the extermination programme itself. They also might have tried to gum up the works, to make the bureaucracies less efficient in their deadly business.

The lesson from Bauman is that we need to pay at least as much attention to the goals of bureaucracies as to their methods. But challenging goals is especially difficult, since there is no formal way to do so. The procedural whistleblower at least has the option of appealing to rules and approaching appeal bodies that are supposed to administer justice (even though they often fail to act against corruption). The goal-related whistleblower has the more overtly political task of challenging the funda-mental direction of the organisation.

In countries occupied by the Nazis, there were many dissi-dents—but not enough. The tragic fact is that the leaders of the most influential institutions—churches, corporations, scientific organisations—did little or nothing to oppose Nazis plans.

Challenging bureaucracy

Whistleblowers have a slim chance of changing a bureaucracy because they are essentially lone critics of a powerful elite. The only real prospect of change comes through collective action, and even this is likely to be a long and difficult process.

In Schweik Action Wollongong, a group with which I've

been involved, we examined seven cases of challenges to bureaucracies.[11]

- The Movement for the Ordination of Women challenged the Anglican Church patriarchy in Sydney.
- Vince Neary blew the whistle on corruption and safety problems in the State Rail Authority of New South Wales.
- At the end of the 1800s, the "modernist movement" within the Roman Catholic Church questioned various aspects of church dogma.
- In the 1970s, attempts were made to reform the repressive prison system in New South Wales.
- Beginning in the 1960s, Dutch soldiers created unions and successfully pushed for better conditions and greater freedoms.
- A massive public movement appeared in the 1980s to oppose the Australian government's plans for a national identity card.
- Women organised for a decade to oppose sexual discrimination at the Port Kembla steelworks of BHP, Australia's largest company.

In each case, we tried to learn lessons from the struggles. Here are our conclusions.

It is extremely difficult to change bureaucracies

Most bureaucratic elites, however corrupt they may be, are never challenged. Bureaucratic elites have enormous power to squash opponents, for example the way the Vatican crushed the Modernists.

---

[11] Brian Martin, Sharon Callaghan and Chris Fox, with Rosie Wells and Mary Cawte, *Challenging Bureaucratic Elites* (Wollongong: Schweik Action Wollongong, 1997; http://www.uow.edu.au/arts/sts/bmartin/dissent/documents/Schweik.cbe/). The group is named after the fictional character Schweik (or Svejk), a soldier who created havoc in the Austrian army during World War I by pretending to be extremely stupid. See Jaroslav Hasek, *The Good Soldier Svejk and his Fortunes in the World War*. Translated by Cecil Parrot. (Harmondsworth: Penguin, 1974).

The challenges that are made usually aim to change policies or personnel, not the structure of bureaucracy itself. The campaign against the Australia Card didn't aim to change the Australian government bureaucracies. It had success in stopping the proposed identity card, but the government's basic goal was achieved through other means.

Sometimes, though, a campaign to change a policy can lead to changes in the bureaucracy. The women's campaign against BHP hiring practices led to a degree of change in the company, namely a less anti-women working environment. This was a significant change, even if the basic hierarchical relationships remained.

A collective challenge is needed

A lone whistleblower like Vince Neary has little chance of success in changing a bureaucracy. Speaking the truth is seldom a good strategy just on its own. It's also necessary to mobilise other supporters on the inside or outside.

The idea that bureaucracies are similar to authoritarian states is a useful one. To challenge an authoritarian state requires a careful strategy. Building support is crucial. Courageous individuals are needed to make open challenges, but these have to be planned in ways that build further support. Some of the methods that can be used in mounting a challenge are:

- careful documentation of problems;
- holding discussions and meetings;
- circulating leaflets and publishing letters and articles;
- liaising with the media;
- building links with outside groups;
- using a variety of methods of nonviolent action, from rallies to pickets and occupations.

The Dutch soldiers' movement carried out its campaigns effectively. By organising a union and operating collectively, the movement accomplished much more than any number of isolated protesters could have. A military bureaucracy is very similar indeed to an authoritarian state, but even states can be toppled through nonviolent action.

An alternative is needed

To have any chance of achieving lasting change, it is vitally important to have an alternative. Most challenges to bureaucratic elites do not even imagine the possibility that there are alternatives to bureaucratic systems, hence they are unlikely to lead to lasting change.

Struggles to change bureaucracy are usually lengthy

The Movement for the Ordination of Women took ten years to change the official policy of the Anglican Church in Australia, and even that was not enough to transform the male-dominated power structure. Attempts to reform prison structures may require decades and there is the constant danger of a reversion to traditional hierarchical systems.

Is it a good idea for activists to make plans for years or decades? Certainly it helps for some to have a long-term vision. But how many people would join a campaign that was expected to last years? Most people get involved with the idea of a quick victory, and some of them then become committed through their experiences. How to build a long-term campaign is a difficult challenge. Bureaucracies by their nature have the long-term commitment of workers, especially the elites. It is far easier to go along with the prevailing way of doing things than to constantly push for change.

Legitimacy is a key to change

If citizens withdraw support, even the most oppressive regime will collapse. Bureaucracies are similarly vulnerable. But just saying "withdraw support" is inadequate. The question is how. Challengers need to understand, through analysis or experience, how the bureaucracy maintains loyalty, how communication systems operate, how links are made with other organisations, how power is exercised against dissent and how people's beliefs and commitments are forged. Not easy! Furthermore, just understanding how the system operates is not enough. It's necessary to know what actions will bring about change.

Action research is needed

There's a great need for study of the process of bureaucratic change from the grassroots, of experimentation with alternative ways of organising work, and of testing out various ways of probing and challenging bureaucracies. Even just raising the idea that bureaucracy is not the only way of organising work is significant. The idea of democratic alternatives to bureaucracies, not just policy or personnel change within bureaucratic structures, needs to be put on the agenda of activists pushing for a more participatory society.

Challenging bureaucracy: the role of information

Elaborating on these lessons, here are some suggestions relating to information. Information is not the only issue, but it is an important one.

Understand the situation

It is vital to be well informed and to have insight into the dynamics of the organisation. If one reacts to injustices solely on the basis of anger or frustration, without a careful analysis of the situation, the danger is that action will be useless or counterproductive.

It can be helpful to read analyses of bureaucracy and about organisations similar to one's own. Even more helpful is to write one's own analysis of what is going on and why. Writing helps to clarify thinking and indeed is a process of thinking. There are many questions to address. Who has power? How is power maintained? What developments are likely in the future? Who can challenge the system? What are the prospects for change?

Have a goal

What is your aim? To rectify a particular problem, or to transform the bureaucracy? Actually, it's possible to combine these, by working on particular issues that, if resolved, help move towards the long-run goal.

One possible goal is "transparent organisations." Activities of any sizeable organisation should be totally open for inspection, whereas the activities of ordinary individuals and small groups should be considered private matters. Similarly, the activities of individuals in positions of power or responsibility should be open for scrutiny, whereas the activities of most people in most circumstances should be considered private matters. For example, a person acting as a delegate representing a large number of people could not expect the same degree of privacy in their delegate role as in other circumstances.

The principle here is that since power tends to corrupt, those with more power (even if only temporarily) must be more open to scrutiny than others. Since organisations typically have more power than individuals, all of their activities should be "transparent"—open to scrutiny by any interested person. This is, in effect, a demand that organisational elites relinquish much of their power over both subordinates and outsiders.

There's a connection here with campaigns against surveillance. In campaigning for transparent organisations, the primary aim is to undermine the legitimacy of organisational secrecy ("privacy" is the wrong word) while maintaining the legitimacy of individual privacy. With less legitimacy, disruption of surveillance systems would come to be considered acceptable, even admirable. Institutional change would become more viable. Workers could organise more effectively. Spy agencies would be under threat. If organisational elites were exposed to intense scrutiny, they would be more likely to favour systems that provided services without discrimination, such as collective provision.

Collect information

Detailed and dependable information is needed about the problems. This can be hard to obtain, since bureaucratic elites prefer to restrict information to those who are trustworthy. Furthermore, when they come under threat, elites may lie, bend the rules and destroy documents. Another big difficulty is disinformation, namely incorrect information that is intentionally spread in order to manipulate opponents or bystanders.

To collect information, it is useful to save documents (including copies in safe places). But it is easy to become overwhelmed by paper or computer files. Just as important as having documents is understanding their significance. Taking notes on events and comparing impressions with others is important.

Spread information

Having information is only a beginning. It's no use if it sits forever on some shelf. To have impact, information needs to be circulated. The general principle in challenging the hoarding of information in bureaucracies is to "spread" it, namely make it available to those who can make use of it.

- Survey results, for example on the morale of workers, can be circulated to all workers.
- Information about hazards to workers can be given to the workers affected.
- Documents showing mismanagement can be distributed to interested people inside and outside the organisation.
- Honest accounts of how the organisation operates can be circulated to everyone.

Anyone who openly circulates information that might damage elites is likely to become a target. Therefore great care needs to be taken in the process of spreading information.

One approach is to circulate information anonymously. This requires extreme caution, such as producing leaflets on word processors and photocopiers that can't be traced, and avoiding leaving fingerprints or even a stray hair. An alternative is to send email messages using anonymous remailers. Even with such precautions, good guesses about who the author is are sometimes possible by close scrutiny of the writing style and the precise information circulated.

Another approach is for an outsider to circulate the information. This could be a journalist, researcher, ex-employee or activist group—preferably someone with nothing to lose if the organisation mounts an all-out attack. The outsider has greater freedom than any insider, but needs reliable information from insiders in order to be a credible commentator.

Sometimes insiders are able to speak out and retain their positions due to personal circumstances or to links with outside supporters. An example is Hugh DeWitt, a physicist at the Lawrence Livermore National Laboratory, a nuclear weapons design lab in California. DeWitt has long been a critic of positions taken by lab managers, for example disputing their arguments against a comprehensive nuclear weapons test ban. On several occasions DeWitt came under attack from the lab management. That he has maintained his position is due in large part to support from prominent figures and activists on the outside.

Mobilise on the inside and outside

The experience of whistleblowers shows that to build a movement for change, support from outside the organisation is essential. To achieve this, reliable information and reliable means of communication are needed.

As long as the struggle takes place inside the organisation, the elites have an enormous advantage since they control financial and human resources as well as the main systems of communication. When the struggle moves outside the organisation, challengers improve their odds.

Employees do not have freedom of speech. If supporters on the outside speak out, it is more difficult to mount reprisals against them. This is the basis for the leak, in which an insider gives information to an outsider, such as a journalist, who can release it without as much risk. Outsiders need insiders as much as vice versa. Only insiders truly understand organisational dynamics. They have the insight into operations and ways of thinking that is essential to developing a sound strategy.

Challenging bureaucracies is no easy task. For workers and clients to transform a bureaucracy into a participatory organisation in which free speech is cherished is one of the great challenges of our age. In spite of so-called "freedom of information," top bureaucrats continue to use information as a means of control. In spite of the rhetoric of democracy and participation, most large organisations are highly resistant to any genuine change. Continued experience in making challenges is vital. Only by repeated attempts can insight be gained into the process of bringing about change. For this, it is important that lessons be learned and communicated to others.

6

Defamation law and free speech

The law of defamation is supposed to protect people's reputations from unfair attack. In practice its main effect is to hinder free speech and protect powerful people from scrutiny. Strategies for people to challenge oppressive uses of defamation law need to be developed.

Defamation law relies on the power of the state—via the courts—to fine those who lose a case. But only those with lots of money need apply. The power behind defamation law is corrupting, which explains why it is so difficult to make even minor reforms to the law to benefit those with little power or wealth.

What it is

The basic idea behind defamation law is simple. It is an attempt to balance the private right to protect one's reputation with the public right to freedom of speech. Defamation law allows people to sue those who say or publish false and malicious comments.

There are two types of defamation.
• Oral defamation—called *slander*—for example comments or stories told at a meeting or party.
• Published defamation—called *libel*—for example a newspaper article or television broadcast. Pictures as well as words can be defamatory.

Anything that injures a person's reputation can be defamatory. If a comment brings a person into contempt, disrepute or ridicule, it is likely to be defamatory.

• You tell your friends that the boss is unfair. That's slander of the boss.

• You write a letter to the newspaper saying a politician is corrupt. That's libel of the politician, even if it's not published.

• You say on television that a building was badly designed. That's libel due to the imputation that the architect is professionally incompetent, even if you didn't mention any names.

• You sell a newspaper that contains defamatory material. That's spreading of a defamation.

The fact is, nearly everyone makes defamatory statements almost every day. Only very rarely does someone use the law of defamation against such statements.

Defences

When threatened with a defamation suit, most people focus on whether or not something is defamatory. But there is another, more useful way to look at it. The important question is whether you have a right to say it. If you do, you have a legal defence.

If someone sues you because you made a defamatory statement, you can defend your speech or writing on various grounds. There are three main types of defence:

• what you said was true;

• you had a duty to provide information;

• you were expressing an opinion.

For example:

• You can defend yourself on the grounds that what you said is true.

• If you have a duty to make a statement, you may be protected under the defence of "qualified privilege." For example, if you are a teacher and make a comment about a student to the student's parents—for example, that the student has been disruptive—a defamation action can only succeed if they can prove you were malicious. You are not protected if you comment about the student in the media.

• If you are expressing an opinion, for example on a film or restaurant, then you may be protected by the defence of "comment" or "fair comment," if the facts in your statement were reasonably accurate.

• There is an extra defence if you are a parliamentarian and speak under parliamentary privilege, in which case your speech is protected by "absolute privilege," which is a complete defence in law. The same defence applies to anything you say in court.

Defamation law varies from country to country. My outline here is oriented to the Australian context where defamation law is considered fairly strict. Even within Australia, the things you have to prove to use one of the defences may not be the same in different parts of the country. For example, in some Australian states, truth alone is an adequate defence. In other states, a statement has to be true and in the public interest—if what you said was true but not considered by the court to be in the public interest, you can be successfully sued for defamation.

What can happen

• You can be threatened with a defamation suit. You might receive a letter saying that unless you retract a statement, you will be sued.

There are numerous threats of defamation. Most of them are just bluffs; nothing happens. Even so, often a threat is enough to deter someone from speaking out or to make them publish a retraction.

• Proceedings for defamation may be commenced against you. This is the first step in beginning a defamation action. Statements of claim, writs or summons shouldn't be ignored. If you receive one, you should seek legal advice.

• The defamation case can go to court, with a hearing before a judge or jury. However, the majority of cases are abandoned or settled. Settlements sometimes include a published apology, sometimes no apology, sometimes a payment, sometimes no payment. Only a fraction of cases goes to court.[1]

The problems

There are several fundamental flaws in the legal system, including cost, selective application and complexity. The result is that defamation law doesn't do much to protect most people, but it does operate to inhibit free speech.

Cost

If you are sued for defamation, you could end up paying tens of thousands of dollars in legal fees, even if you win. If you lose, you could face a massive pay-out on top of the fees.

The large costs, due especially to the cost of legal advice, mean that most people never sue for defamation. If you don't have much money, you don't have much chance against a rich opponent, whether you are suing them or they are suing you. Cases can go on for years. Judgements can be appealed. The costs become enormous. Only those with deep pockets can pursue such cases to the end. If you have say $100,000 or more to risk, go ahead and sue. Otherwise defamation law is not *for* you—though it might be used *against* you.

The result is that defamation law is often used by the rich and powerful to deter criticisms. It is seldom helpful to ordinary people whose reputations are attacked unfairly.

Unpredictability

People say and write defamatory things all the time, but only a very few are threatened with defamation. Sometimes gross libels pass unchallenged while comparatively innocuous comments lead to major court actions. This unpredictability has a chilling effect on free speech. Writers, worried about defamation, cut out

---

[1] In Australia and the US, perhaps one out of five suits goes to trial: Michael Newcity, "The sociology of defamation in Australia and the United States," *Texas International Law Journal,* Vol. 26, No. 1, Winter 1991, pp. 1-69.

anything that might offend. Publishers, knowing how much it can cost to lose a case, have lawyers go through articles to delete anything that might lead to a legal action. The result is a tremendous inhibition of speech.

Complexity

Defamation law is so complex that most writers and publishers prefer to be safe than sorry, and do not publish things that are quite safe because they're not sure. Judges and lawyers have excessive power because outsiders cannot understand how the law will be applied. Those who might desire to defend against a defamation suit without a lawyer are deterred by the complexities.

Slowness

Sometimes defamation cases are launched years after the statement in question. Cases often take years to resolve. This causes anxiety, especially for those sued, and deters free speech in the meantime. As the old saying goes, "Justice delayed is justice denied."

In Australia, a common sort of defamation case brought to silence critics is political figures suing, or threatening to sue, media organisations. The main purpose of these threats and suits is to prevent further discussion of material damaging to the politicians. Other keen suers are police and company directors. People with little money find it most difficult to sue.

Defamation law definitely affects the mass media, having a chilling effect on free speech. There is a direct chill when stories are changed or spiked. More deeply, there is a structural chill when areas are not investigated at all because the risks of libel suits are too great.[2]

The examples in this chapter are Australian, where defamation laws are notorious for their severity and their use against free

---

2 Eric Barendt, Laurence Lustgarten, Kenneth Norrie and Hugh Stephenson, *Libel and the Media: The Chilling Effect* (Oxford: Oxford University Press, 1997).

speech, and where there is no clear constitutional protection for free speech. In the US, things would appear to be better, with explicit constitutional free speech protection and a public figure defence against defamation. But the US legal system can still be used against those who speak out. In the early 1980s, two Denver University academics—law professor George Pring and sociology professor Penelope Canan—joined together to investigate a rash of cases in which legal charges were made against citizens who spoke out in one way or another.[3] For example, citizens

- testified at a hearing about a real estate development
- wrote a letter to the Environmental Protection Agency about pollution
- made a complaint about police brutality
- collected signatures for a petition
- reported law violations to health authorities.

In these and many other such cases, the citizens were sued by the real estate developer, the company complained about to the EPA, the member of the police, etc. The most common charge was defamation, but also used were business torts (such as interference with business), conspiracy, malicious prosecution and violation of civil rights. Pring and Canan dubbed these cases Strategic Lawsuits Against Public Participation or SLAPPs. These suits have very little chance of success and in practice very few actually succeed. However, they are very effective in scaring the targets, most of whom become much more cautious about speaking out.

Pring and Canan realised that a key to resisting SLAPPs was constitutional protection for the right to petition the government—an often overlooked part of the first amendment to the US Constitution. By emphasising the free speech and constitutional aspects of these cases, and just by calling them SLAPPs, it is much easier to resist and sometimes to win suits against the SLAPPers for malicious prosecution. Pring and Canan's book is

---

3 George W. Pring and Penelope Canan, *SLAPPs: Getting Sued for Speaking Out* (Philadelphia: Temple University Press, 1996).

an essential guide for anyone threatened with a SLAPP. Yet the very prevalence of SLAPPs in the US shows that constitutional protection alone is not enough to prevent the use of the law to suppress free speech. For the reasons outlined here, such as complexity and cost, the legal system is a battleground that is biased in favour of those with more power and wealth. Greater formal protection by the law does not necessarily translate into greater freedom of speech in reality.

Media power and defamation

One of the best responses to defamatory comments is a careful rebuttal. If people who make defamatory comments are shown to have gotten their facts wrong, they will lose credibility. But this only works if people have roughly the same capacity to broadcast their views.

Only a few people own or manage a newspaper or television station. Therefore it is difficult to rebut prominent defamatory statements made in the mass media. Free speech is not much use in the face of media power. There are cases where people's reputations have been destroyed by media attacks. Defamation law doesn't provide a satisfactory remedy. Apologies are usually too late and too little to restore reputation, and monetary pay-outs do little for reputation.

Most media organisations avoid making retractions. Sometimes they will defend a defamation case and pay out lots of money rather than openly admit being wrong. Media owners have resisted law reforms that would require retractions of equal prominence to defamatory stories.

By contrast, if you are defamed on an electronic discussion group, it is quite easy to write a detailed rebuttal and send it to all concerned the next hour, day or week. Use of defamation law is ponderous and ineffectual compared to the ability to respond promptly. Promoting interactive systems of communication as an alternative to the mass media would help to overcome some of the problems associated with defamation.

Examples

These examples are all Australian because they are the ones I'm most familiar with. I need to know each case reasonably well to avoid defamation! There are plenty of similar examples from other countries.

• Physicist Alan Roberts wrote a review of a book by Lennard Bickel entitled *The Deadly Element: The Men and Women Behind the Story of Uranium.* The review was published in the *National Times* in 1980. Bickel sued the publishers. He was particularly upset by Roberts' statement that "I object to the author's lack of moral concern." There was a trial, an appeal, a second trial, a second appeal and a settlement. Bickel won $180,000 in the second trial but received a somewhat smaller amount in the settlement.[4]

• Sir Robert Askin was Premier of the state of New South Wales for a decade beginning in 1965. It was widely rumoured that he was involved with corrupt police and organised crime, collecting vast amounts of money through bribes. But this was never dealt with openly because media outlets knew he would sue for defamation. Immediately after Askin died in 1981, the *National Times* ran a front-page story entitled "Askin: friend to organised crime."[5] It was safe to publish the story because, in Australia, dead people cannot sue. (In some countries families of the dead can sue.)

• In 1992, students in a law class at the Australian National University made a formal complaint about lecturer Peter Waight's use of hypothetical examples concerning sexual assault. Waight threatened to sue 24 students for defamation. Six of them apologised. Waight then sued the remaining 18 for $50,000 for sending their letter to three authorised officials of

---

4 David Bowman, "The story of a review and its $180,000 consequence," *Australian Society,* Vol. 2, No. 6, 1 July 1983, pp. 28-30.

5 David Hickie, "Askin: friend to organised crime," *National Times,* 13-19 September 1981, pp. 1, 8

the university. He later withdrew his suit. Subsequently the students' original letter of complaint was published in the *Canberra Times* without repercussions.[6]

• In 1989, Tony Katsigiannis, as president of the Free Speech Committee, wrote a letter published in the Melbourne *Age* and the *Newcastle Herald* discussing ownership of the media. Among other things, he said of a review of the Broadcasting Act "that its main concern will be to save the necks of the Government's rich mates." Although he mentioned no names, he and the newspaper owners were sued for defamation by Michael Hutchinson, a public servant who headed the review of the Broadcasting Act. Hutchinson sued on the basis of imputations in the letter, which can be judged defamatory even when not intended by the writer. Hutchinson said he wouldn't accept just an apology; he wanted a damages payment and his legal costs covered. Katsigiannis received $20,000 worth of free legal support from friends, but after three exhausting years of struggle he agreed to a settlement in which he apologised but Hutchinson received no money.[7]

• In 1985 Avon Lovell published a book entitled *The Mickelberg Stitch*. It argued that the prosecution case against Ray, Peter and Brian Mickelberg—sentenced to prison for swindling gold from the Perth Mint—was based on questionable evidence. The book sold rapidly in Perth until police threatened to sue the book's distributor and any bookseller or other business offering it for sale. The Police Union introduced a levy on its members' pay cheques to fund dozens of legal actions against Lovell, the distributor and retailers. The defamation threats and actions effectively suppressed any general availability of the book. For ten years, none of the suits against Lovell reached

[6] Graeme Leech, "Lecturer drops suits against students," *Australian,* 28 April 1993, p. 13; Andrea Malone and Sarah Todd, "Facts and fiction of the Waight saga," *Australian,* 5 May 1993, p. 14.

[7] Robert Pullan, *Guilty Secrets: Free Speech and Defamation in Australia* (Sydney: Pascal Press, 1994), pp. 27-28.

trial, but remained active despite repeated attempts to strike them out for lack of prosecution. Eventually, in 1996 Lovell reached a settlement with the Police Union. All the cases were dropped and he became free to sell his books in their original form. (Financial details of the settlement are confidential.)[8]

• In the late 1970s, fisherman Mick Skrijel spoke out about drug-running in South Australia. Afterwards, he and his family suffered a series of attacks. The National Crime Authority (NCA) investigated Skrijel's allegations but in 1985 ended up charging Skrijel for various offences. Skrijel went to jail but was later freed and his sentence set aside. In 1993, the federal government asked David Quick QC to review the case; Quick recommended calling a royal commission into the NCA, but Duncan Kerr, federal Minister for Justice, declined to do so. Skrijel prepared a leaflet about the issue and distributed it in Kerr's electorate in Tasmania during the 1996 election campaign. Kerr wrote to the Tasmanian media saying he would not sue Skrijel but that he would sue any media outlet that repeated Skrijel's "false and defamatory allegations." The story was reported in the *Financial Review* but the Tasmanian media kept quiet.[9] Skrijel's view is that most media wouldn't have published much on his case no matter what and that defamation law provides a convenient excuse for media not to publish.

Options

In practice, the court system and the media serve to protect the powerful while doing little to protect the reputation of ordinary people. They undermine the open dialogue needed in a democracy. There are various options for responding to uses of defama-

---

8 Avon Lovell, *The Mickelberg Stitch* (Perth: Creative Research, 1985); Avon Lovell, *Split Image: International Mystery of the Mickelberg Affair* (Perth: Creative Research, 1990).

9 Richard Ackland, "Policing a citizen's right to expression," *Financial Review,* 9 February 1996, p. 30.

tion law to silence free speech. Each has strengths and weaknesses.

Avoid defamation

Writers can learn simple steps to avoid triggering defamation threats and actions. The most important rule is to *state the facts, not the conclusion.* Let readers draw their own conclusions.

• Instead of saying "The politician is corrupt," it is safer to say "The politician failed to reply to my letter" or "The politician received a payment of $100,000 from the developer."

• Instead of saying "The chemical is hazardous," it is safer to say "The chemical in sufficient quantities can cause nerve damage."

• Instead of saying, "There has been a cover-up," it is safer to say "The police never finalised their inquiry and the file has remained dormant for nine years."

Be sure that you have documents to back up statements that you make. Sometimes understatement—saying less than everything you believe to be true—is more effective than sweeping claims.

If you are writing something that might be defamatory, it's wise to obtain an opinion from someone knowledgeable. (Remember, though, that lawyers usually recommend that you *don't* say something if there's even the slightest risk of being sued.)

Another way to avoid being sued for defamation is to produce and distribute material anonymously. Some individuals do this with leaflets. They are careful to use printers and photocopiers that cannot be traced. At times when few people will notice them, they distribute the leaflets in letterboxes, ready to dump the remainder if challenged. Gloves of course—no fingerprints. For those using electronic mail, it's possible to send messages through anonymous remailers, so the receivers can't trace the sender.

These techniques of avoiding defamation law may get around the problem, but don't do much to eliminate it. They illustrate that defamation law does more to inhibit the search for truth than foster it. If an anonymous person circulates defamatory material about you, you can't contact them to sort out discrepancies.

Say it to the person

Send a copy of what you propose to publish to people who might sue. If they don't respond, it will be harder for them to sue successfully later, since they haven't acted to stop spreading of the statement. If they say that what you've written is defamatory, ask for specifics: which particular statements or claims are defamatory and why? Then you can judge whether their objections are valid.

It's not defamatory to criticise a person to their face or to send them a letter criticising them. It's only defamation when your comments are heard or read by someone else—a "third party."

Keep a copy for posterity

If you have to censor your writing or speech to avoid defamation, keep a copy of the original, uncensored version—in several very safe places. Save it for later and for others, perhaps after all concerned are dead. You might also inform relevant people, especially those who might threaten defamation, that you have saved the uncensored version. (Be aware, though, that you might be called to produce this material as part of the discovery process in a defamation action!)

Defamation law distorts history. How nice it would be to read old newspapers in uncensored versions, if only they existed! By saving the unexpurgated versions, you can help challenge this whitewashing of history.

Call the bluff

If you are threatened with a defamation action, one strategy is to just ignore it and carry on as before. Alternatively, invite the threatener to send the writ to your lawyer. Most threats are bluffs and should be called. The main thing is not to be deterred from speaking out. The more people who call bluffs, the less effective they become.

If you receive a defamation writ, try to find a lawyer who is willing to defend free speech cases at a small fee or, if you have little money, no cost. Shop around for someone to defend you or contact public interest groups for advice.

Use publicity

Just because you are sued doesn't mean you can't say anything more. (Many organisations avoid making comment by saying that an issue is *sub judice*—that is, under judicial consideration—but that's just an excuse.) You can still speak. In particular, you can comment on the defamation action itself and its impact on free speech. It's also helpful to get others to make statements about your case.

A powerful response to a defamation suit is to expand the original criticism. Defamation suits aim to shut down comment. If enough people respond by asserting their original claims more forcefully and widely, this will make defamation threats counterproductive.

A group called London Greenpeace produced a leaflet critical of McDonald's. McDonald's sued five people who were involved in distributing it. Two of them, Helen Steel and Dave Morris, decided to defend themselves—they had no money to pay lawyers. They used the trial to generate lots of publicity. Because of the trial—the longest in British history—their leaflet has reached a far greater audience than would have been possible otherwise. The whole exercise has been a public relations disaster for McDonald's.[10]

Law reform recommendations

Law reform commissions have been advocating reform of defamation law for decades. Possible changes include:
- public figure defence so that it's possible to make stronger criticisms of those with more power;
- adjudication outside courts, to reduce court costs;

---

[10] http://www.mcspotlight.com; John Vidal, *McLibel* (London: Macmillan, 1997).

- elimination of monetary pay-outs, requiring instead apologies published of equal prominence to the original defamatory statements.

In spite of widespread support for reform among those familiar with the issues, Australian law remains much the same. That's because it serves those with the greatest power, especially politicians who make the law and groups that use it most often.

Reforms sometimes don't help as much as planned. The US has a public figure defence, for example, which means that suers must prove malice. This has become the pretext for highly intrusive discovery exercises that can themselves deter free speech. Fixing the law is at most part of the solution. It's also necessary to change the way the legal system operates.

Campaigns for reform of the legal system

Any change that makes the system cheaper, speedier and fairer is worth pursuing. The sorts of changes required are:

- reducing costs that are excessive compared to damage done or large compared to a party's income;
- allowing court orders to remove tax deductibility for the legal costs of corporations assessed to have acted highhandedly;
- making laws simpler;
- introducing compulsory conciliation;
- speeding up legal processes.

There's a much better chance of change when concerned individuals and groups organise to push for change. This involves lobbying, writing letters, organising petitions, holding protests, and many other tactics. In the US, campaigning by opponents of SLAPPs has resulted in some states passing laws against SLAPPs.

Set up defamation havens

The World Wide Web creates the possibility of undermining the use of defamation law to suppress free speech. There are cases in which documents that are defamatory in one country have been posted on web sites in other countries where it is harder and more inconvenient to sue.

If a country decided to abolish its defamation law, it could become a defamation haven, namely a safe place to post documents on the web that could be read throughout the world. Local writers could volunteer to author such documents or indigent writers in other countries could do it. There are no such defamation havens yet but, like tax havens, becoming one could become lucrative for some small countries.

In the spirit of free speech, managers of web sites that publish controversial material can offer to post responses. The best remedy for defamatory statements is a timely response. This is quite easy to arrange on the Internet.

Speak out campaigns

Petitions, street stalls and public meetings can be used to directly challenge the use of defamation law against free speech. One possibility is to circulate materials that have been subject to defamation threats or writs. Another is to protest directly against those who attempt to use defamation law to suppress legitimate comment. If enough people directly challenge inappropriate uses of the law, it will become harder for it to be used. Freedom of speech is a product of social action, not of law.[11]

Conclusion

Defamation law doesn't work well to protect reputations. It prevents the dialogue and debate necessary to seek the truth. More speech and more writing is the answer to the problem rather than defamation law, which discourages speech and writing and suppresses even information that probably wouldn't be found defamatory if it went to court. Published statements—

---

[11] David Kairys, "Freedom of speech," in David Kairys (ed.), *The Politics of Law: A Progressive Critique* (New York: Pantheon Books, 1982), pp. 140-171.

including libellous ones—are open, available to be criticised and refuted. The worst part of defamation law is its chilling effect on free speech. It has a corrupting influence on the powerful, who use defamation threats and actions to deter or penalise criticism. The availability of defamation law in its present form encourages powerholders to suppress criticism rather than openly debate the critics.

The most effective penalty for telling lies and untruths is loss of credibility. Systems of communication should be set up so that people take responsibility for their statements, have the opportunity to make corrections and apologies, and lose credibility if they are repeatedly exposed as untrustworthy. Defamation law, with its reliance on complex and costly court actions for a tiny fraction of cases, doesn't work.

Defamation actions and threats to sue for defamation are often used to try to silence those who criticise people with money and power. The law and the legal system need to be changed, but in the meantime, being aware of your rights and observing some simple guidelines can help you make informed choices about what to say and publish.

In the long run, the aim should be to establish a series of processes that foster dialogue and honesty, without giving anyone excessive power over others. This can include replacing mass media with interactive media, enabling free speech by workers, and transforming or replacing systems that allow surveillance, as described in earlier chapters. As well, there might be "reputation mediators," to advise disputants on contentious claims. There might be voluntary "reputation tribunals" that would make statements about contested claims after receiving testimony and documents. A tribunal's credibility would depend on its perceived independence, fairness and promptness. With these and other possibilities, there would be no power to invoke financial or other punitive sanctions. The main tool would be speech itself.

7

The politics of research

The work of professional researchers is strongly influenced by funding, disciplines, hierarchy and competition. As a result, it is mainly useful to corporations, governments, professions and researchers themselves. Strategies to challenge this pattern include critical teaching and research, popularisation and community participation in research.

Economists have devoted huge amounts of effort into developing models of capitalist economies. There are enormous computer models of economies used to assess the impact of a change in tariffs or investment. Large amounts of data on employment, interest rates and the like are collected and analysed. Econometricians—economists who look at abstract models of economies—have developed entire bodies of mathematical analysis.

Most economists give very little attention to anything that challenges their fundamental assumptions. John Blatt, a leading applied mathematician, examined some of the assumptions underlying neoclassical economic models—such as the assumption that an economy will tend toward equilibrium—and found that they did not hold up.[1] His work should have led to a reexamination of the foundations of neoclassical economics. Instead, it was ignored.

---

[1] John M. Blatt, *Dynamic Economic Systems: A Post-Keynesian Approach* (Armonk, NY: M. E. Sharpe, 1983).

Gandhian economics, based on local self-reliance and simplicity in living, is based on completely different assumptions to standard economic theory.[2] Gandhian economics is studied in India and Sri Lanka but virtually unknown in most other countries.

In summary, it could be said that economic knowledge is oriented to certain powerful groups, notably corporations, governments and economists themselves. Other disciplines are not much different, in that they too are oriented to powerful groups—though often different ones.

The word "knowledge" suggests certainty, authoritativeness, even usefulness. It is a good thing to be knowledgeable. Yet much knowledge is quite limited, specific, parochial. Chemists working for pharmaceutical companies seek knowledge about how to make tablets dissolve faster. Military engineers develop better armour for tanks. Psychologists investigate connections between brain structure and the behaviour of rats.

Knowledge isn't necessarily everlasting, nor is it necessarily of general value. Rather than thinking of knowledge as great truths engraved on tablets in the sky, it's more useful to think of knowledge as ideas that are generally agreed by specific communities. Scientific knowledge, for example, is what the bulk of relevant specialists agree on at any particular time. Knowledge can change, for example ideas about mechanisms of evolution or the development of continents. Knowledge can be biased in various ways, for example by providing a restricted picture of economic behaviour.

There are all sorts of knowledges: an auto mechanic's knowledge of motors, a parent's knowledge of a child, a person's knowledge of the position of their own body, a small community's knowledge of interpersonal relationships, a mass audience's knowledge of statements in the mass media, and

---

2 See, for example, Amritananda Das, *Foundations of Gandhian Economics* (Bombay: Allied Publishers, 1979).

many others. Here my focus is on the sorts of knowledge that
have greatest credibility in most First World societies, namely
knowledge certified by scientists, engineers, medical researchers, lawyers and other such experts.

In this chapter I begin by outlining some of the ways that
interest groups affect the creation and use of knowledge, such
as through funding, disciplines, hierarchy and competition.
Then I examine some strategies for moving towards a more
participatory and egalitarian connection between power and
knowledge.

The shaping of knowledge

An old saying is that "The one who pays the piper calls the
tune." This applies to knowledge as much as to anything else. If
a pharmaceutical company sponsors research into drugs to
reduce tension or control hyperactivity, then that is what the
researchers are likely to find if they are successful. Funding
alone doesn't guarantee results, of course, but if something is
found it is likely to be of more value to the funder than others.
The drug researchers might, in the course of their investigations,
happen upon a substance that does something different, such as
preventing kidney stones. But they are unlikely to do much
research on unpatentable substances or methods, since there's no
profit in that. They certainly won't find a way to reduce tension
that doesn't involve drugs at all, such as by relaxation, biofeed-
back or small group dynamics, since they are looking only at
drugs.

Funding, then, doesn't force results but it provides a strong
steering process. Only certain types of knowledge are likely to
result because the researchers are paid to look only for certain
types of things.

Funding for the majority of formal research in the world
today is provided by governments and corporations. The amount
of funding from trade unions, churches, environmental groups or

women's groups is tiny by comparison. That means that most research follows governmental or corporate agendas.[3]

Military research is a big proportion. Here the aim is to develop more powerful weapons, more precise guidance systems, more penetrating methods of surveillance, and more astute ways of moulding soldiers to be effective fighters. For the researchers, the tasks can be very specific, such as designing a bullet that is more lethal—or sometimes less lethal, for crowd control purposes. Many talented scientists have devoted their best efforts to making weaponry more deadly.

In most government and corporate labs, practical relevance to the goals of the organisation is highly important. In these labs, the direct influence of groups with different agendas is minimal. Environmental groups do not expect chemical corporations to do research into biological control as an alternative to pesticides, and do not bother to lobby for such a change. Groups with little money to fund research turn instead to universities.

Overall, university research is less targeted to specific outcomes than most government and corporate research. This is especially true of fields like philosophy and mathematics. But before getting carried away by the wonders of "pure research" in universities, a bit of context is needed.

Universities were originally set up to train ministers and lawyers who were part of the privileged classes. Over the centuries, different groups have pushed to have universities serve their own purposes. Business leaders want graduates who will be committed and hard-working employees. Leaders of the legal, medical and other professions want training to reproduce the profession. Governments want training for prospective civil

---

3 David Dickson, *The New Politics of Science* (New York: Pantheon, 1984); Janice Newson and Howard Buchbinder, *The University Means Business: Universities, Corporations and Academic Work* (Toronto: Garamond Press, 1988); James Ridgeway, *The Closed Corporation: American Universities in Crisis* (New York: Random House, 1968); Thorstein Veblen, *The Higher Learning in America: A Memorandum on the Conduct of Universities by Business Men* (New York: B. W. Huebsch, 1918).

servants. Parents want opportunities for their children. Social movements look for scholarly support for their agendas. The university is a focal point for these and other pressures and agendas.[4]

No single group has been able to control universities for its own purposes. If, for example, corporate leaders decided to run universities themselves, it would cost a lot of money. They would come under attack from other groups with conflicting agendas, such as parents and professional elites. The consequence has been that most universities are funded wholly or partly by governments but retain a considerable degree of autonomy compared to corporate or government research labs. The belief in "academic freedom" for scholars to pursue teaching and research provides a convenient way for universities to appear to serve the general interest while still catering for those with more power and money.

The training of members of professions remains a key task for universities. The majority of students and staff in most universities are in specific applied areas, such as medicine, law, accountancy and engineering. Research in these fields tends to be oriented to the priorities of the wider profession. Medical researchers are far more likely to investigate surgical treatments of haemorrhoids than prevention of haemorrhoids by change of diet. There is scope for research in a variety of directions, but there are several pressures towards a service orientation, including outside funding (for example by medical supply companies), controls by certification bodies (needed to vouch that a degree is suitable preparation for becoming a doctor), possible jobs outside the university, and the expectations of colleagues.

A few fields are not so tightly tied to outside groups, notably the natural sciences, social sciences and humanities. This includes disciplines such as physics, biology, sociology and

[4] Margaret Scotford Archer, *Social Origins of Educational Systems* (London: Sage, 1979).

history. Even in these areas there is the possibility of outside funding that influences research agendas. It might seem that biologists and historians are in a good position to undertake research that serves groups without money to directly pay for research. A few of them do, but not many. There are other factors to consider. Not least is the self-interest of academics themselves.

Most universities are divided up into units according to what are called disciplines, from architecture to zoology. The names and sizes of units vary from place to place. Some universities have a single mathematics department, others have pure mathematics, applied mathematics, and statistics. Occasionally new disciplines emerge and break off, such as computer science. The important point, though, is that members of each discipline jealously guard their own little patch of knowledge. They attempt to control teaching of students in their discipline, appointments in the field and the type of research that is published in the field's central journals.

Disciplines are based around a framework for understanding the subject matter of the field. Students are trained in the standard way of thinking. If researchers work in a university setting, they are influenced by colleagues. If they want to publish scholarly papers, they have to get past referees, who are usually established members of the field, most of whom expect research to follow the standard patterns. Referees and editors expect authors to be familiar with standard ideas and publications in the field, which requires a considerable investment of effort to comprehend. All this prevents outsiders from waltzing in to make a contribution to the discipline. To use another metaphor, disciplinary expectations operate like strong tariff barriers against moving very far from one's own training and previous research output.

So far, then, I've discussed two major factors that influence the production of knowledge: funding and disciplines. Sometimes these reinforce each other. For example, a civil engineer working for a government roads authority will be primarily oriented to the practicalities of road design and construction, but may maintain a link to the engineering profession through journals and conferences, perhaps even writing papers for conference proceedings.

On the other hand, sometimes funding and disciplinary influences pull in different directions. Many practical problems cannot be dealt with effectively within one discipline. For example, the development of an effective military strike force requires skills from manufacturing, economics, psychology, organisational dynamics and other areas. Discipline-based universities are not much use for pulling these areas together; think-tanks, with teams of many different specialists and generalists working together, are more likely to be helpful. Little bits of the larger problem can be farmed out to specialist researchers.

	Plenty of funding	**Little funding**
Disciplines	chemical engineering, computer science, accountancy, law	philosophy, history, creative writing
Inter-disciplinary fields	policy making, military planning, corporate strategies	peace studies, women's studies, political economy

There is quite a bit of disagreement about what constitutes a discipline. In fact, there is ongoing tension and conflict in universities over boundaries between disciplines. Usually it is those who deal with theory—pure mathematicians, theoretical physicists, econometricians—who lay claim to the core of the discipline. Others are simply "applying" the knowledge. The theory-application or pure-applied tension results from the two dimensions of influence in the above table, funding and disciplines. Power for disciplines comes from control over ideas, hence the status and influence of theory. Most money comes directly or indirectly from the potential for applications, but this makes researchers more dependent on outside groups. This creates the curious situation in universities in which theoreticians have the greatest status but applied work reaps the greatest material rewards.

The areas that are most commonly left out in the cold are interdisciplinary fields for which there is little funding. By the logic of disciplines, these fields are simply ignored. Only when there is a popular movement do universities sometimes find that there is an area of study worthy of attention. For example, the rise of the environmental movement in the 1960s led many universities to set up environmental studies programmes. But because these programmes didn't fit neatly into disciplinary boxes, they were vulnerable to cutbacks and amalgamations as the years wore on.

If disciplines are thought of as fiefdoms based on monopolies over separate bodies of knowledge, this helps to explain a number of features of academia.[5] If the members of the discipline claim that they alone are qualified and knowledgeable to make decisions about the discipline, then it is helpful if it is difficult for outsiders to understand what is going on. Jargon fits in here. The specialised language and concepts of the discipline are convenient for those in the know. They also are convenient for ensuring that outsiders can't quickly see through to the essence of the issues.

Research is the process of testing existing knowledge and developing new knowledge. Research is generally rarefied and accessible only to specialists. Hence, it bolsters disciplines, since disciplines are essentially based on claims built around bodies of knowledge.

By contrast, teaching is a process of helping others to understand bodies of knowledge. Teaching is necessary to reproduce the discipline by training new recruits, but if it makes the core of

---

5 For critiques of some disciplines, see for example Stanislav Andreski, *Social Sciences as Sorcery* (New York: St. Martin's Press, 1973); Trevor Pateman (ed.), *Counter Course: A Handbook for Course Criticism* (Harmondsworth: Penguin, 1972).

the discipline seem too easy or obvious, then it can undermine the credibility or mystique of the discipline. It should be no surprise, then, that in most universities research has far more status than teaching. Teaching is problematic for a discipline— necessary, but potentially threatening.

More definitely threatening is popularisation, namely making ideas of the discipline readily accessible to a wide audience. Popularisation undermines the mystique of the field, helping outsiders to gain insight into central areas. Many academics look down on popularisers even when such individuals are accom- plished scholars. Ironically, some popularisers serve their disci- plines by building public support. But just as theory is venerated in universities although most funding comes for applications, so esoteric research contributions are lauded whereas those who are popular with students and the wider public are greeted with suspicion. The latter are a threat because they have a power base not controlled by the discipline itself.

One more factor is vital in this complex situation: hierarchy. Not everyone doing research is equal. At the top are directors of research institutes, university managers and editors of presti- gious journals. Research hierarchies seldom are straight up and down like in the military, but involve a complex array of positions. A researcher can be influential through supervising many research students, heading a department, sitting on a research grants committee, being an official in a professional association, or editing a journal. The figures who combine many of these roles are powerful in the discipline.

Hierarchy helps to orient research to sources of funding and to disciplinary priorities. The more powerful researchers often have personal or professional links with powerful figures in funding organisations. Junior researchers who might be tempted to stray from conventional research topics are brought into line by the competition for positions, funding and status. To get a job, to get research grants, to get promotions, it is highly advantageous to follow the beaten track, innovating enough to distinguish oneself from others but not so much as to threaten the existing system of knowledge. Most prominent popularisers are senior figures who have already established their scholarly reputations and have secure jobs. Younger scholars keep their heads down.

Education for hire?

From the point of view of the classical ideals of higher education, which can be summarised by the phrase "the pursuit of truth," modern higher education has many failings.

- Knowledge is treated as a commodity, passively accepted and absorbed by student consumers.
- Classroom experience is organised around the premise that learning results only from being taught by experts.
- Knowledge is divided into narrow disciplinary boxes.
- Original, unorthodox thoughts by students, and nonconventional choices of subjects and learning methods, are strongly discouraged.
- Competition prevails over cooperation.
- Knowledge and learning are divorced from social problems or channelled into professional approaches.
- Credentials, the supposed symbols of learning, are sought more than learning itself.
- Performance in research takes precedence over commitment to teaching.
- Most research is narrow, uninspired and mediocre, useful only to other experts or vested interests.
- Scholarly openness and cooperation take second place to the academic rat race and power struggle which involves toadying, backstabbing, aggrandisement of resources and suppression of dissidents.
- Original or unconventional thoughts by staff, or action on social issues, are penalised, while narrow conformist thought and action are rewarded.

The existing system of knowledge production is quite complex, but understanding its main features explains a lot.₆ It can be summarised as follows. Funding in particular areas and for particular applications is of fundamental importance in government and corporate research laboratories. Within the university sector, funding is important but so are disciplines. Knowledge production and teaching are divided up according to disciplines and research specialties. Some disciplines are closely tied to particular professions, but disciplinary elites have a great deal of power. Finally, hierarchy within research communities keeps most junior researchers in line. The essence of the academic system is remarkably stable in spite of periodic upheavals. Although funding, disciplines and hierarchy help to orient most research to groups with more money and power, the system is not totally controlled. Researchers sometimes align themselves with goals and groups outside the mainstream.

Intellectuals on their own are not major wielders of power. They mostly operate to serve other powerful groups, especially governments, corporations and professions, by providing useful knowledge and by providing legitimacy for policies and practices.⁷ For example, engineers do their job to help improve roads, factories, electricity systems and computer networks, and thus serve transport departments, industrial enterprises, electricity authorities and computer companies. By being the experts in designing such systems, they provide legitimation for the

---

6 Some good treatments—all of US higher education—are J. Victor Baldridge, *Power and Conflict in the University: Research in the Sociology of Complex Organizations* (New York: Wiley, 1971); Theodore Caplow and Reece J. McGee, *The Academic Marketplace* (New York: Basic Books, 1958); Lionel S. Lewis, *Scaling the Ivory Tower: Merit and its Limits in Academic Careers* (Baltimore: Johns Hopkins University Press, 1975); Arthur S. Wilke (ed.), *The Hidden Professoriate: Credentialism, Professionalism, and the Tenure Crisis* (Westport, CT: Greenwood Press, 1979).

7 Charles Derber, William A. Schwartz and Yale Magrass, *Power in the Highest Degree: Professionals and the Rise of a New Mandarin Order* (New York: Oxford University Press, 1990).

process, in which nonexperts have little say unless they are key figures in the relevant organisation.

Social activists often express great frustration and annoyance with academics who are in such a good position to help the cause but do so little. A tenured academic has job security, a good salary, flexible working hours and a great deal of control over areas to research—not to mention, in many cases, specialist knowledge and considerable skills in writing and speaking. Such a person could be a tremendous asset to a hard-pressed activist group dependent on volunteers and without the capacity to carry out in-depth investigations. While quite a few academics sympathise with environmental, peace, feminist, antiracist and other social movements, very few become heavily involved. Hence the frustration.

Activists do not get so annoyed at nonsupportive researchers in corporations and governments, since the constraints on them are greater and much more obvious. In universities, there are fewer formal constraints. But the pressures for proper academic behaviour are quite powerful: funding, job opportunities, training in the discipline, peer pressures. The chains are more subtle and more easily broken, but they do exist.

Corruptions of expert knowledge

Knowledge isn't power just by itself, but it can be a means for obtaining power, wealth and status. Because of this, individuals and groups try to convince others that they have exclusive access to the truth—in other words, that they are the authorities in particular areas of knowledge. In order to part with this knowledge, they ask for fees, jobs, careers and status. Because there can be money and status from being a recognised expert, there is a temptation for experts to sell themselves to the highest bidder. Many experts are willing to serve those who are powerful, who are not necessarily those who need expert knowledge the most.

Once a group of experts has established itself as having exclusive control over a body of knowledge, it is to their advantage to exclude nonexperts. This occurs in many ways. A long and expensive training is commonly demanded before a newcomer can be accepted as an expert. In the case of medicine, law, engineering and some other professions, formal certification is required in order to practise in the field. The new recruit is expected to use the appropriate jargon. Editors expect a certain approach and type of writing for contributions to expert journals.

Most experts are full-time professionals. Those who might like to make an occasional contribution are not made welcome. Finally, many experts are arrogant, displaying contempt or hostility to amateur interlopers.

Full-time professional experts are not inherently nasty. Rather, the power they gain from having control over the field leads them to develop attitudes, beliefs, training systems and procedures that maintain the control and keep out nonexperts.

Occasionally outsiders try to enter the expert domain. Alternative health practitioners make recommendations on preventing and treating disease. Home buyers handle legal details themselves rather than hiring a lawyer. Citizen groups oppose planning decisions recommended by engineers. In cases such as this, the challengers can come under attack. Doctors try to get government support to outlaw medical advice by anyone without a medical degree. Lawyers try to restrict legal practice to their own members. Engineers attack the credibility of citizen interveners.

Sometimes the challengers know as much—have as much "expertise"—as the official experts. The conflict is between the expert establishment, namely the group of experts with official recognition and more power, versus expert outsiders.[8]

Even more serious is when an expert who is part of the establishment becomes a dissident, questioning the standard way of doing things. A doctor who questions the value of chemotherapy

---

[8] Brian Martin (ed.), *Confronting the Experts* (Albany: State University of New York Press, 1996).

or an accountant who exposes corporate corruption is liable to come under attack, being harassed, ostracised, reprimanded, demoted and dismissed. Instead of responding to the person by discussing the issues and attempting to refute their views, the dissident becomes the target. This can only happen when the establishment has power that can be exercised against dissidents.

An alternative vision

The existing system for producing knowledge is based on funding, from those who can afford it, for full-time professionals to carry out research that is communicated to peers in specialist journals. This system powerfully shapes visions of alternatives. Most of those who want to change the system want some of the research to be oriented towards problems that concern them. They are concerned about bias in research results, not about questioning underlying biases in the research system.

An alternative model of research is community participation and control. Community participation means that anyone potentially could join in research projects: no credentials would be required. Community control means that funding and accountability would be in the community's hands.

Model:	Elite	Community
funding	governments, corporations	community
participation	professional researchers	volunteers
organisation	hierarchy	egalitarian
knowledge	disciplines	problem-oriented

Some academics argue that they should be given full academic freedom, without constraints from government and corporate funders. But this is really just a claim for funding without accountability. The community model does not eliminate controls over knowledge production. The question is the nature of the controls and who can participate in research.

The community model is such a complete challenge to the elite model that it is hard to see how it might operate. It is basically a vision of an alternative, not a prescription for changing things right now. There are a few suggestive pointers.

- Trials have shown that high school students can, after a few months of training, do publishable medical research.[9]
- Groups of citizen researchers in Japan have carried out innovative studies of pollution, for example tracking down the source of Minamata disease sooner than high-powered professional research teams.[10]
- Numerous citizen groups carry out "community research," involving community members in studies of health, social services, and various other topics.

Science is one of the most highly professionalised aspects of modern society. While there are quite a few talented amateur botanists and astronomers, there are hardly any amateur physicists or mechanical engineers. Therefore it is especially difficult to see what an alternative would look like without the system as it exists. There might well be massive investment in a community-run research system, and many of the same people might spend much of their time doing research.

To begin to imagine the community model of research, it is necessary to imagine a different economic structure. One example is a system where the basic necessities of life are available to everyone in the community as a matter of right: food, clothing, shelter, transport. Those who wanted to would be able to work in areas of their choosing, subject to availability of facilities and opportunities. Some might choose to spend most of their time in a single area, such as building houses or rearing children. Others might choose to be active in a variety of areas,

---

[9] The programme run by Gary Huber is described in "Bucking the system," *Newsweek,* 10 January 1972, p. 26.

[10] Jun Ui, "The interdisciplinary study of environmental problems," *Kogai—The Newsletter from Polluted Japan,* Vol. 5, No. 2, Spring 1977, pp. 12-24.

such as growing food, producing appliances and painting. This picture is sketchy, to be sure, but is one possible way to organise society that is compatible with what is known about human psychology and skills.

What is today called research could be undertaken in a variety of situations. Those working in a particular area, such as producing plastics, teaching history or designing transport systems, could undertake investigations as part of doing their work better. They might do the investigations themselves or invite others to undertake them. Others might feel like undertaking research independently of work situations, either on their own or in groups.

There could be just as much research in a society organised this way as in current societies. Curiosity is a common human trait, especially in children. Given the opportunity, many more people might become involved in some sort of research. Large-scale projects would be possible by communities agreeing to make funds available. There would be big differences, though, in the power associated with expert knowledge. Rather than a small elite making the crucial decisions about research and most research being oriented to powerful groups, in this hypothetical society the power associated with expert knowledge would be greatly reduced. Entry into research activities would be much easier. Community members would be more involved in making decisions about what research should be undertaken, what facilities should be funded, etc.

My point is not to advocate this particular picture of community research. It is just one of many visions.[11] Rather, my aim is to suggest that the corruptions of power associated with expert

---

[11] See also Peter Abbs and Graham Carey, *Proposal for a New College* (London: Heinemann Educational Books, 1977); Bill Draves, *The Free University: A Model for Lifelong Learning* (Chicago: Association Press, 1980); Jonathan Kozol, *Free Schools* (Boston: Houghton Mifflin, 1972); Michael P. Smith, *The Libertarians and Education* (London: Allen and Unwin, 1983).

establishments should be recognised and taken into account when designing a research system. No doubt it will take a fair bit of experimentation—research!—to determine what sort of system can most effectively produce knowledge that serves the common interest.

What can be done?

There are lots of possible ways to challenge the orientation of knowledge to powerful groups, and many people are making challenges in their own way. There's no single best strategy, because what a person can do depends on their own situation. So it's worth looking at a range of possibilities.

Critical teaching

Teaching is inherently a threat to academic control over bodies of knowledge, since the aim is explaining ideas to wider audiences. If teaching is kept pretty much to the straight and narrow, covering orthodox ideas, then it's not a threat. Getting students to think for themselves and to question conventional wisdom in a fundamental way potentially undermines intellectual privilege.[12]

The usual limitation of critical teaching is that it remains critical at the level of ideas. There are some powerful critiques of orthodox theory available, but they just sit on the shelves or in students' essays unless someone does something about them. The priority of most students is to obtain degrees. If given encouragement, they might write a hard-hitting essay, but sending a letter to a local newspaper is another story.

There are, though, some enterprising teachers and even entire departments that promote learning by getting students actively engaged in community issues, for example tackling pollution problems or providing legal help to minority groups.

---

[12] Ira Shor, *Critical Teaching and Everyday Life* (Montreal: Black Rose Books, 1980).

Critical research

Although the bulk of research carried out is directly or indirectly oriented to the interests of dominant groups (including the researchers themselves), some researchers explicitly aim their work in other directions. This includes engineers who develop appropriate technology for disadvantaged people and psychologists who seek ways for people to resist manipulation by advertisements.

A lot of "critical research" that is published in academic journals is never read by anyone except academics. It is too abstract and difficult to read for anyone else. More helpful is critical research that engages with people, providing a product or idea that can be grasped and used.

Critical teaching and research merge when students are involved in projects that essentially involve doing research as a means of learning. So-called "action research" can fit this picture. Researchers, including students, undertake projects that help communities to help themselves, such as working with homeless people to develop strategies against policies creating homelessness.

Popularisation

When knowledge is kept within professional circles it is mainly of service to those who have the money or power to get professionals to do their bidding. Making the knowledge understandable to a wider community undermines the professional monopoly. No wonder that popularisers are looked down upon by experts in their fields.

There are different types of popularisation. Some popularisers, such as Isaac Asimov, Martin Gardner and Carl Sagan, mainly speak of the wonders of science. Their popular works mainly serve to get more people to support scientific work by the professionals. They seldom make criticisms of powerful patrons of science. (Sagan's prominent role in promoting the theory of nuclear winter and arguing for nuclear disarmament may be a partial exception.) Other popularisers, such as Rachel Carson,

David Suzuki and John Kenneth Galbraith, have taken a more critical role: they encourage people to be critical of influential trends in their fields.

Only a small number of individuals can ever become as widely known as Sagan and Suzuki. But others can undertake the task of critical popularisation in their own way. For example, political scientist Michael Parenti has written many books providing a straightforward, hard-hitting critique of the US political and economic system. These books have had far more impact than sophisticated critiques published in left-wing journals mainly read by a few left-wing intellectuals.

Independent scholarship

Rather than taking the road through universities—namely, formal study and acquisition of credentials—it is possible to learn and do research outside the academic system. So-called "independent scholars" are people who have learned or researched on their own, in some cases becoming prominent as a result. Examples include Betty Friedan, Buckminster Fuller, Hazel Henderson, Eric Hoffer, Alvin Toffler and Barbara Tuchman.[13]

Independent scholars are not so shaped by formal training, peer expectations, and organisational penalties for going against the grain. On the other hand, independence in many cases means getting little money from one's intellectual efforts, or else becoming dependent on a new patron, such as the publisher of a commissioned book.

Research and social movements

Feminists, environmentalists and other social activists vary enormously in the way they use research. I've met some environmental campaigners who never read a single political analysis. They act entirely on the basis of their own experience of how the political system operates. Some research is important

---

[13] Ronald Gross, *The Independent Scholar's Handbook* (Berkeley, CA: Ten Speed Press, 1993).

to them, such as detailed analyses of threatened species in local forests or the comparative social impacts of transport policies, if it directly relates to current campaigns.

A few campaigners read deeply into theory on relevant topics such as patriarchy, capitalism, industrialism and the dynamics of social movements. Some of them have told me that the writings in these fields are insightful but seldom relevant to the actual campaigns on which they are engaged.

Imagine for a moment that social movements could spend billions of dollars funding research relevant to their interests and needs. This would lead to a considerable change in research priorities. Whereas coal companies fund research into more efficient ways of extracting and burning coal, environmental groups might fund research into measures for energy efficiency and how to promote them. Whereas militaries fund research into more powerful and accurate weapons, peace groups might fund research into conflict resolution or nonviolent struggle.

But would this mean that most researchers would still be professionals working in universities or specialist research organisations? Would it mean that decisions about research funding and priorities would still be made by just a few people in the social movements and among the researchers? If so, problems similar to the present system might arise, namely orientation of research to the interests of those with most power.

The challenge is (1) to involve a broad cross-section of people in decision making about research priorities and (2) to allow all interested people to be engaged in research themselves, at some level. To meet this challenge, social movements need to put research on their agendas.[14]

---

[14] On education and social movements, see Colin Ball and Mog Ball, *Education for a Change: Community Action and the School* (Harmondsworth: Penguin, 1973); Tom Lovett, Chris Clarke and Avila Kilmurray, *Adult Education and Community Action: Adult Education and Popular Social Movements* (London: Croom Helm, 1983); Michael Newman, *Defining the Enemy: Adult Education in Social Action* (Sydney: Stewart Victor, 1994).

8

On the value of simple ideas

Rather than building complex social theory and then drawing conclusions for making a better society, it is more productive to find, develop and promote simple ideas that empower people and then build up theory that is compatible with these ideas.

Simple ideas have a bad reputation. People often think simple ideas are simplistic: wrong, incomplete, inaccurate, misleading. I agree that many simple ideas are no good, but many are quite useful. This is easy to overlook because complex, sophisticated systems of knowledge are thought to be better.

The usual scholarly approach to knowledge goes like this. Sophisticated models of atoms, mental processes, society or whatever are proposed, analysed, elaborated, tested and negotiated. The best available model is then used to draw conclusions. If appropriate, it is applied to practical problems. This usually means lots of the complexities have to be ignored. The simple, practical version of the theory is never as good as the fully elaborated version.

The areas of knowledge that especially interest me are theories about how to make society more just and equal, in particular to eliminate various forms of domination. There's lots of high-brow theory about this. Most social science journals, for example, are theoretically daunting. The jargon can be frightening enough on its own, and the ideas expressed by the jargon often do not make much sense to outsiders. Consider, for example, the following impressive sentence:

> "It's TV then, not just as a technical object which we can hold apart from ourselves, but as a full technical ensemble, a social apparatus, which implodes into society as the emblematic cultural form of a relational power, which works as a simulacrum of electronic images recomposing everything into the semiurgical world of advertising and power, which links a processed world based on the exteriorisation of the senses with the interiorisation of simulated desire in the form of programmed need-dispositions, and which is just that point where Nietzsche's prophetic vision of twentieth-century experience as a 'hospital room' finds its moment of truth in the fact that when technique *is* us, when TV is the real world of postmodernism, then the horizon finally closes and freedom becomes synonymous with the deepest deprivals of the fully realized technological society."[1]

If you are brave enough to criticise the analysis, a common response is that "you don't really understand." Occasionally some pearls of wisdom for activists come down from the great scholars. What is one to make of these, not really understanding where they came from?

In summary, the usual procedure for many intellectuals is to first develop a good theory and then work out its implications. To be sure, there is a lot of talk about the importance of "learning from practice," namely not theorising in a vacuum. The key thing, though, is the great importance put on developing a good theory. Simple interpretations of complex theory are denigrated,

---

[1] Arthur Kroker, "Television and the triumph of culture: three theses," *Canadian Journal of Political and Social Theory,* Vol. 9, No. 3, Fall 1985, pp. 37-47, at p. 37.

as in the case of "vulgar Marxism." My argument is that this emphasis is wrong.

Simple ideas and associated actions should be the centre-piece, the foundation for theoretical development. The goal should be to develop effective actions and simple, effective ideas to go along with them. Sophisticated theory should be built up in a way that is compatible with the simple ideas.

Simple ideas

Simple ideas are ones that are relatively easy to understand, communicate and use. Some simple ideas in our society are

- money,
- roundness of the earth,
- birthdays,
- melodies,
- telephones.

Most people (at least in industrialised societies) are familiar with these things at an elementary level.

Needless to say, most people do not understand their full complexities. Not many people are familiar with advanced bodies of knowledge associated with these simple ideas, such as

- econometric modelling,
- geophysical measurement techniques,
- the origins of the calendar,
- musicology,
- electronic engineering.

Unfortunately, even the concept of a simple idea isn't all that simple! What's simple for one person to understand may be quite difficult for another. What is simple depends on experiences, formal education, social class, mass media, gender, and many other factors. Nevertheless, I'm going to proceed using "simple ideas" as a simple idea, trying not to get bogged down in complexities.

Michael Schudson in a book on advertising makes some points about how products are democratised. These points also apply to ideas.

- "First, they become more standard as they come to be produced for a mass audience. They are easier to handle, easier to 'do it yourself' without great skill on the part of the user; both a mediocre cook and a great cook make equally good cakes from a cake mix."
Simple ideas are like this. Anyone can grasp them and use them to get results.

- "Second, products become not only more standard but milder and easier to use." Children can grasp and apply the ideas.

- "Third, there is democratization when goods are consumed in increasingly public ways."[2] When people use ideas at work or in discussions on the bus, they have been "democratised," and this commonly happens only for simple ideas. For example, the idea that bodies and behaviours are influenced by genetic factors is becoming ever more widely used, especially when media stories tell of genes for alcoholism or aggressiveness. Biologists may cringe when they hear inaccurate interpretations of genetic theory, but there is no doubt that the simple version is widely used.

Just because I'm commenting on the value of simple ideas doesn't mean that what I have to say is simple itself. Because I'm questioning the standard way of thinking about ideas, what I have to say may be hard to grasp at first. I'll do my best to explain it.

Most intellectuals, I'm convinced, think in terms of quite simple models. But few of them express themselves equally simply, since that would undermine their credibility as sophisticated, even great, thinkers.

---

[2] Michael Schudson, *Advertising, the Uneasy Persuasion* (New York: Basic Books, 1984), p. 181.

Here, in outline, is my basic idea:

- The most important thing is developing effective methods of action and simple ideas to think about them.

- Theory should be built up around these simple ideas.

* * *

The usual approach is shown in this diagram. Sophisticated theory is shown as a cloud of concepts, relationships, puzzles, interactions. Below the cloud are a few spin-offs for action, often based on a simplified version of complex theory. This might be called the trickle-down model of theory and action.

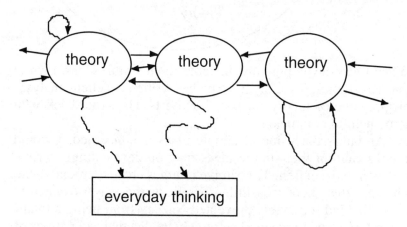

Some bodies of theory are so esoteric that there are no obvious spin-offs: the cloud can float along without much application at all. A large amount of current work on poststructuralism—which involves "deconstructing" standard concepts—seems to fit this description.[3]

---

[3] A good critique is Barbara Epstein, "Why poststructuralism is a dead end for progressive thought," *Socialist Review,* Vol. 25, No. 2, 1995, pp. 83-119.

An alternative approach is to develop a solid set of practices and simple ideas, and develop theory that is compatible with it.

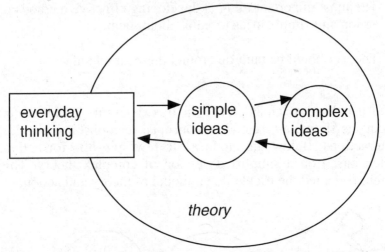

When I was developing my thoughts about simple ideas, I wrote to Chris Rootes, a sociologist who has written excellent analyses of the value of theory for social activists. He wrote back with some helpful comments:

"As far as the value of simple ideas is concerned, I would simply caution that simple ideas may be devastatingly wrong and even have extremely coercive regimes erected around them. The fact that there was little enough in the way of coherent theory behind it scarcely prevented Nazism from being a totalitarian force, and very simple, scarcely intellectualised notions of race or nation have been perfectly adequate to motivate some of the nastiest regimes in history. I think maybe 'common sense' whether it be of the liberal or the conservative sort has much to recommend it because at least it allows people to behave decently toward one another."

This was helpful advice. Simple ideas can be helpful to murderous regimes and lead to disastrous policies. I certainly didn't want to suggest that all simple ideas are good.

Later, I was talking about this to Carl Hedman, a philosopher and community activist living in Milwaukee, Wisconsin. He immediately solved the problem. He said, "Of course not all simple ideas are valuable. But some of them are. The task is to find the ones that are helpful for socially beneficial purposes." A logician would say that simplicity is a necessary condition but not a sufficient one.

That's basically my argument. Rather than judging ideas according to sophisticated theory, we should judge sophisticated theory according to whether it builds on and contributes to simple ideas that are helpful in practice for achieving the things we value.

Case studies

I've picked out a number of examples that show the value of certain simple ideas, even though in some ways the ideas are misleading, incomplete or even just plain wrong. These examples are just illustrations. No doubt some of them can be interpreted differently or used to draw different lessons. New information or analysis may invalidate them. There are lots of other possible examples; each person needs to find the ones most appropriate for them.

Sexual harassment

For untold decades, women have suffered a range of unwelcome behaviours by men. These include verbal comments of a sexual nature ("hey bitch!"), staring at breasts or crotch, touching and grabbing, demands for sexual favours (sex in order to get or keep a job), sexual assault and rape. Most women learned how to ignore or avoid these behaviours. The boss who made crude sexual jokes, leaned closely over one's shoulder, patted one's backside and grabbed a kiss when everyone else had gone home was just part of the job.

The resurgence of the feminist movement in the 1960s led women to reexamine their lives. The term "sexual harassment" was coined to refer to a variety of behaviours that are unwelcome, unsolicited and unreciprocated. The idea of sexual harassment captured the experiences of many women. The term was soon used widely and campaigns began to stop it, by telling women that they didn't have to put up with it, by setting up committees to deal with complaints and by passing legislation against it. Sexual harassment still continues to occur, but it is increasingly stigmatised and resisted.

"Sexual harassment" has become a simple idea, a name for a common problem that once had no name. Like all simple ideas, there are difficulties with the idea of sexual harassment. Does a sexually explicit photograph on a shopfloor wall constitute sexual harassment? Do the perpetrators have to be told that their behaviour is unwelcome? Does a single incident count as sexual harassment, or does it require repeated instances? These and other questions can be answered according to particular sexual harassment policies or legislation. There are deeper questions, though. For example, does it make sense to include such a wide range of behaviours—from staring and casual touching to assault and rape—under one category?

Two feminist activists and scholars, Sue Wise and Liz Stanley, wrote a detailed critique of the idea of sexual harassment. Their basic theme is that sexual harassment has been defined in a narrow fashion that leaves out the harassment of women in everyday life and ignores women's practical means of resistance. They show that "sexual harassment" has been packaged in a framework oriented to the workplace in which blatant acts of harassment are dealt with through formal mechanisms. They use anecdotes and arguments to illustrate more commonplace forms of harassment and some practical ways of responding to them. They argue that the conventional idea of sexual harassment presents women as victims, with men as the saviours via formal procedures. They argue instead that women should take action themselves. They argue that idea of sexual harassment doesn't really grapple with the problem of male domination.[4]

I think Wise and Stanley's critique is superb. They have wonderful insights. They have shown weaknesses in the concept of sexual harassment. Nevertheless, for all its weaknesses, I still think "sexual harassment" is a useful concept because it helps people understand everyday problems and enables campaigns to be mounted against undesirable behaviours. "Sexual harassment" may be flawed as a concept but it is still quite useful. For practical purposes, replacing it with a more sophisticated conception of male domination would not necessarily be better.

Quantum theory

In the 1920s, theoretical physicists developed powerful new ways to describe the behaviour of atoms and their component parts such as protons, neutrons and electrons. Models from the everyday world didn't seem to apply all that well. One standard model is the particle: in some ways an electron behaves like a tiny billiard ball with an electric charge. In other ways, though, an electron behaves more like a wave, for example in causing diffraction patterns. Quantum physicists developed a mathematical way of explaining both these behaviours, symbolised by Schrödinger's equation.

Many physicists are happy just to use the equations to work out energy levels and other results. Some ask, though, what the equations mean. Physicists in the 1920s largely reached agreement on one particular interpretation—the so-called Copenhagen interpretation—of the equations. This interpretation is based on indeterminism. The wave function in Schrödinger's equation provides a set of probabilities for where a particle might be, but the actual position is not determined until there is an observation, causing a collapse of the wave function.

In the 1930s, the talented mathematician John von Neumann proved that a deterministic interpretation of

---

[4] Sue Wise and Liz Stanley, *Georgie Porgie: Sexual Harassment in Everyday Life* (London: Pandora, 1987).

Schrödinger's equation, using hidden variables, was not possible. For most physicists this proof was irrelevant, since they considered the matter closed anyway.

Then in 1952 along came physicist David Bohm. He developed a deterministic, hidden-variable interpretation of quantum theory. This was impossible according to von Neumann. It wasn't until 1966 that a flaw was found in von Neumann's proof. Bohm had already shown, through practical example, that the proof didn't apply. As in many cases, doing the impossible is easier than proving that a theory is wrong.

Quantum theory has caused many a physics student perplexity and anguish. Of greater interest, though, is the widespread interest in quantum theory among critics of social institutions. The Newtonian model of the universe—rule-bound, predictable, regular—has long been used as a metaphor for society. The classical physicist's orderly universe underpins an orderly society in which everyone knows their place and keeps things running smoothly. If nature is "really" orderly, then it's appropriate that society is too, so the logic goes.

Some members of the new social movements of the 1960s looked to quantum theory for a different inspiration. If nature is inherently unpredictable and interactive, then this is a better model for society. Fritjof Capra in *The Tao of Physics* argued that quantum theory has strong analogies to eastern mysticism.[5] Writers on political theory, psychology, and social change have looked to quantum theory for inspiration.

Personally I don't think it makes much sense to apply ideas from quantum theory to society. After all, the Copenhagen interpretation is just one interpretation, though admittedly the dominant one. Alternatives exist, such as Bohm's hidden variable theory. One historian of science argues that if things had been a bit different in the 1920s, a hidden variable interpretation

5 Fritjof Capra, *The Tao of Physics: An Exploration of the Parallels between Modern Physics and Eastern Mysticism* (London: Flamingo, 1992, 3rd edition).

might have triumphed then.[6] The use of quantum theory to inspire insights into society is built on quicksand.

Does this matter? The application of models from science to society is always a process of simplification. The theory of evolution is another example. Darwin's analysis of natural selection was corrupted and simplified into "the survival of the fittest." Darwinian ideas applied to economics and the social sphere are used to justify capitalism. By contrast, quantum theory applied to social arenas is usually used to criticise established institutions. In my view, whether ideas are true scientifically is largely irrelevant when they are applied to society. Quantum theory can validly be used for inspiration, but not for justification of any particular perspective on society.

One way to proceed is to start by picking what we think are desirable characteristics of society, such as self-reliance, freedom, compassion and innovation. Then we can look at nature, whether at other species or subatomic particles, for analogies to these characteristics. These analogies may then provide ideas for understanding or promoting the desirable characteristics of society. The key is to use simple ideas about society and nature for our purposes.

The consent theory of power

What is power? I'm concerned here with social power or political power, not power as defined in physics. Most people think of power as something that is possessed. It can come through wealth, formal position (president, general, corporate director, pope), sometimes charisma. Powerful people have it—they are the "powerholders." Powerless people don't have much. In this perspective, the struggle for power is a struggle for the levers to control others, such as money and position.

For those who want to help create a more just and equal society, this picture is not very hopeful. It suggests that the best

---

[6] James T. Cushing, *Quantum Mechanics: Historical Contingency and the Copenhagen Hegemony* (Chicago: University of Chicago Press, 1994).

way to bring about change is to capture power in order to make improvements. This of course is the standard strategy adopted by reformers, who attempt to rise in government bureaucracies, to promote election of progressive political parties and to adopt enlightened stands in professional associations. The danger is that the process of seeking power tends to corrupt the leaders of the progressive movements. As progressives attempt to obtain power in order to change social institutions, they are changed sooner than the institutions.

There is, though, a different perspective on power that is much more suited for challengers. This is the consent theory of power. The basic idea is that people don't hold power—rather it is ceded to them by others. In short, people give their consent to being ruled. If they withdraw their consent, then even the most ruthless ruler will be powerless.

Gene Sharp is the world's most influential living writer on nonviolent action. (Only Gandhi, who died in 1948, is as influential.) He analysed the dynamics of nonviolent action and catalogued 198 different methods of nonviolent action—including many varieties of strikes, boycotts, symbolic action, sit-ins, etc.—each with historical examples. Sharp's analysis is built on the consent theory of power, which he has modified, elaborated and applied for the purposes of understanding how nonviolent action works.[7]

Sharp's development of the consent theory of power has had a big impact among nonviolent activists. It has been taught in workshops to thousands of activists as the way to understand power in society. It is linked to more practical training in group dynamics, campaign planning, and preparation for direct action.

In spite of his enormous influence among activists, Sharp's ideas have had minimal impact among political scientists. The consent theory of power has little scholarly support. I am a

---

[7] Gene Sharp, *The Politics of Nonviolent Action* (Boston: Porter Sargent, 1973); Gene Sharp, *Social Power and Political Freedom* (Boston: Porter Sargent, 1980).

supporter of nonviolent action but, having looked at other sorts of analyses, I also was not so sure about the consent theory. So I undertook a closer study of the theory.[8] I concluded that the theory is flawed because it doesn't take into account social structures. Most people cannot simply "withdraw consent" because they are enmeshed in complicated systems in which they are partly under the authority of others and partly have authority over others. Furthermore, in systems where power is "built in" to mechanisms—such as the market in capitalism—there are no obvious rulers from whom to withdraw consent. The consent theory is most plausible when there is an obvious ruler, such as a military dictator, and is less plausible in more complicated systems of power.

I concluded that the consent theory of power is deeply flawed. Intellectuals could probably tear it to shreds if they wanted to, but they ignore it since it has no visibility in scholarly circles. In spite of its theoretical weaknesses, the consent theory is admirably suited for activists. It is just what they need to give them both insight and hope that taking action will make a difference. Moreover, the theory is not applied in a vacuum. There are activists who have an acute intuitive grasp of local political realities. For these activists, the theoretical weaknesses of the consent theory don't matter so much.

For activists, the consent theory is a simple idea. It basically says, "you can make a difference by withdrawing consent from dominant interests." It makes sense of what activists do and what they want to achieve. It is a theory that is tied to a particular type of action. A more sophisticated theory, such as Althusser's structural theory of ideology or Gramsci's theory of hegemony, would not necessarily be more useful.

---

[8] Brian Martin, "Gene Sharp's theory of power," *Journal of Peace Research,* Vol. 26, No. 2, 1989, pp. 213-222. See also Kate McGuinness, "Gene Sharp's theory of power: a feminist critique of consent," *Journal of Peace Research,* Vol. 30, No. 1, 1993, pp. 101-115.

The usual academic approach is to build a comprehensive analysis of society and then see what implications this has for action. In the case of theories of power, I think it makes more sense to start with nonviolent activists and build theories on the basis of what they are doing. The consent theory is a good place to start.

Yes, I know that the very idea of "nonviolent action" is problematic theoretically. That's another area where I think it's better to build theory around action.

Oral sepsis

In the early 1900s, the theory of oral sepsis gained great support among British dentists. "Oral sepsis" or "focal sepsis" was the idea that many diseases gain entry to the body through bad teeth. In retrospect, the theory was wrong and was never supported by very much good evidence. Two authors who studied the reception to the theory, Gilles Dussault and Aubrey Sheiham, say that "the acceptance of a medical theory by practitioners and by the public is as much determined by social and economic factors as by its scientific validity or its therapeutic potential."

William Hunter, the British doctor who developed the theory, used it to attack conservative dentistry that was done mainly in the United States. Hence more research was done on it in the US and more opposition to it was expressed there. Although it ended up being wrong, oral sepsis theory helped draw attention to oral hygiene and gum disease and improved restorative techniques. Dussault and Sheiham conclude "In the end, the example of oral sepsis shows that even an unfounded theory can produce beneficial results."[9]

This is not unusual in science. The most important theories are the ones that stimulate productive research, and many

---

9 Gilles Dussault and Aubrey Sheiham, "Medical theories and professional development: the theory of focal sepsis and dentistry in early twentieth century Britain," *Social Science and Medicine,* Vol. 16, 1982, pp. 1405-1412, quotes from pp. 1405, 1410.

theories that do this are later shown to be false. Oral sepsis theory also illustrates that theories can be adopted or adapted to serve the needs of those who use them.

SLAPPs

In West Virginia in the 1970s, farmer Rick Webb made a complaint to the US Environmental Protection Agency about pollution of a river by a coal company. The company responded by suing Webb for defamation, asking for $200,000. In 1983, a number of residents in a small town in Colorado signed a formal petition for a referendum to stop conversion of some farmland for residential development. Four of those who signed the petition were sued by the developer for "an undetermined amount."

Two academics at the University of Denver, Penelope Canan and George Pring, became aware of an epidemic of legal actions of this sort. The basic pattern was for a company to use the courts to intimidate citizens who were simply exercising their constitutional right to petition the government. The actions for defamation, conspiracy, judicial process abuse and other legal claims had little chance of success and hardly ever succeeded when they did go to court, but that didn't matter. They often were quite successful in scaring citizens, many of whom backed off from their activities.

Canan and Pring carried out extensive studies of this development. They dubbed these suits Strategic Lawsuits Against Public Participation or SLAPPs.[10] The basic concept was that the law was being used to quell free speech. The idea of SLAPPs caught on very quickly. There were many articles in law journals, some of them proposing slightly different definitions than Canan and Pring's. More importantly, the idea of SLAPPs was immensely helpful to the citizens who were being sued. It

---

[10] George W. Pring and Penelope Canan, *SLAPPs: Getting Sued for Speaking Out* (Philadelphia: Temple University Press, 1996). See chapter 6 for another context.

helped them understand what was happening and to formulate a better informed response. Canan and Pring used their knowledge and contacts to mobilise opposition to SLAPPs around the US, including laws against them passed in a number of states.

It is possible to quibble with the definition of a SLAPP, to debate whether particular types of cases fit the model and to question the usual strategies used against them, such as the countersuit or SLAPP-back. Potential complexities abound. Nevertheless, the basic idea of a SLAPP is simple and captures enough of people's experience to be extremely useful. The acronym SLAPP is brilliant and seems to have helped a lot.

Strategy against nuclear power

In Australia, the peak years of debate over nuclear power were 1975-1984. Much of the debate focused on uranium mining, since Australia has large deposits of uranium and plans for nuclear power plants had never progressed very far.

In 1983, four of us in Friends of the Earth Canberra decided to write an article about strategy against nuclear power.[11] We planned our article as an analysis of the deep-rooted driving forces behind the nuclear fuel cycle followed by an assessment of various strategies in the light of our analysis. We had lots of debates about "driving forces" and eventually ended up concentrating on four: the state, capitalism, patriarchy and the division of labour. The strategies we examined were lobbying, participating in environmental inquiries, working through the trade union movement, working through the parliamentary system and grassroots mobilisation. We concluded that grassroots mobilisation—including such things as leaflets, talks, petitions, marches, promoting nuclear-free zones, and civil disobedience—offered the best prospects for challenging the social structures behind nuclear power.

---

[11] The article appeared as a booklet in January 1984. An abridged version was published as Friends of the Earth (Canberra), "Strategy against nuclear power," *Social Alternatives*, Vol. 5, No. 2, 1986, pp. 9-16.

We sent a draft of our article to quite a few people in the antinuclear movement, asking them for comments. This was revealing. Quite a number of them said they agreed with our conclusions but disagreed with certain parts of our analysis—but each person had a different disagreement with the analysis.

When we wrote the paper, we imagined that the analysis and the conclusions were logically linked together. But the responses suggested something else, namely that the same strategy could be justified by a range of different analyses. It almost seemed that the analysis didn't matter all that much: the key thing was the strategy.

We wrote our paper in the usual fashion, putting the analysis first and then using the analysis as a means of assessing strategy. Yet if readers disagreed with the analysis, the risk was that they wouldn't persevere to the section on strategy.

This experience got me thinking about the connection between theory and practice. Our discussion of theories of the state, capitalism, patriarchy and so forth was presented in simple terms, without much elaboration, and in close connection with a practical analysis of the development of nuclear power. If our down-to-earth discussion of theory was contentious for activists, what about the jargon-filled treatments in scholarly books and journals? I knew the answer to that question. They are almost totally irrelevant for activists. Most sophisticated theory is too complex, too qualified and too remote from applications to be of much practical use. The only exceptions are when there is a simple version.

Theories of technology

Many people used to think that technology is always a good thing. The development of nuclear weapons undermined that view. On the other hand, a few people think technology is generally bad, but this view is hard to justify when thinking of hoes or hearing aids.

The most common view is that technology is neutral and so

can be used for good or bad. This is called the use-abuse model. The idea is that technology can be *used* (for good purposes) or *abused* (for bad purposes). Another common idea about technology is that it has a momentum of its own: once a technology such as the car or the telephone gets started, it can't be stopped. This is called technological determinism.

Social analysts who focus on technology rejected all these ideas long ago. In university classes where I work, we spend lots of time explaining why technology is not neutral and why technological determinism is wrong. Currently, a favourite view among scholars in the field is constructivism. In this model, technologies are the outcome of diverse social processes, including world views, prior technologies, organisational structures, social class, etc. There is no inevitability. Neutrality is an irrelevant concept. Instead, individual technologies have to be studied in the context of the circumstances in which they are conceived, developed, opposed, altered, instituted and superseded.

There are some highly sophisticated analyses of technology available. But there is a big problem. The more sophisticated theories don't provide a simple way of thinking about technology. Admittedly, some scholars can become accustomed to thinking in terms of actor-networks in which people, platypuses and paint brushes are all equivalent "actors" in an undifferentiated struggle to get their way. But this seems suited mainly for scholarly analyses, not for practical dealings with technology.

I'm almost inclined to advocate simplistic ways of thinking about technology. Rather than neutral technology, I prefer the idea of biased technology. Some technologies, such as cluster bombs, are biased towards bad uses; others, such as straw hats and solar hot water collectors, are biased towards benign uses.

In addition, it may not matter all that much what general theories of technology people espouse, since what counts is their response. In spite of the prevalent belief in technological determinism, there have been major campaigns against technologies such as nuclear weapons, supersonic transport aircraft and pesticides. If people really believed that technologies couldn't be stopped, why would they bother campaigning against or for them? If they really believed that technologies are neutral, why would they care whether electricity is produced by wind, coal, hydro or nuclear power? For most activists, scholarly theories of technology are unknown and irrelevant, for better or worse I'm not sure. I do think that theories of technology are more relevant when they were grounded in readily understandable and practical ideas.

Conclusion

These examples suggest a number of points.

- Sometimes a wrong idea can be more useful than a correct idea. A wrong idea sometimes can be a good way of pursuing the truth.
- Sometimes getting the theory right doesn't really matter for practice. Rather than being the basis for practice, a theory may just be used to justify practice.
- Some simple ideas are useful for producing a good society, but many of them are irrelevant or harmful.

Many intellectuals do not take kindly to these points. Whenever I've suggested that it doesn't really matter all that much whether theory is right, I've encountered all sorts of objections. "Surely it's better to base practice on a theory that is logically consistent, coherent and complete. It only makes sense that an improved analysis will lead to improved practice."

I'm not convinced. Just because a theory is self-consistent, for example, doesn't necessarily mean it is more useful for activists than a self-contradictory one. That's because knowledge is always incomplete. Forcing a theory to be consistent may eliminate insights and dynamism. From the point of view of some future improved theory, "consistency" may just mean forcing the theory into a straitjacket based on an ill-considered assumption.

This doesn't mean that inconsistency is better. It means that getting the theory right is not the first priority, but simply one thing to do among others. Of equal or greater importance is promoting ideas that are relevant to practice and that can be simply understood.

There are plenty of simple ideas around, and lots of them are used to prop up sexism, racism, poverty and the like. In order to challenge simple ideas used for oppressive purposes, it's valuable to promote simple ideas that encourage human ideals. But this is not an easy task.

It is one thing to come up with a simple idea that is an improvement over what's available. But promoting it is a different story. There are stacks of people in advertising, for example, who devote their careers to developing catchy slogans or striking images that will sell. They are experts on attaching products to cultural stereotypes. Toys, for example, are increasingly differentiated by gender, with Barbie for girls and He-Man for boys and a host of others. Gender stereotypes are widely understood and thus can be used as an effective marketing strategy.[12]

This sort of corporate use of simple ideas is essentially manipulative. It is not aimed at helping people understand their lives, but rather getting them to buy a product. Most mainstream political uses of simple ideas, such as politicians' campaign pitches about crime or debt, are similarly manipulative.

Finding, developing and promoting simple ideas that empower people is quite a challenge. The ideas of SLAPPs and sexual harassment are instructive. These ideas speak to people's experiences, enabling them to understand problems confronting them and encouraging them to take action.

Promoting simple ideas can be a struggle. Dominant groups often attempt to discredit ideas. The idea of "anarchy" in

---

[12] Wendy Varney, *The Social Shaping of Children's Manufactured Toys* (forthcoming).

principle means society without government but is widely used as a synonym for chaos. This is largely due to attacks by capitalists, politicians and communists. Anarchists consequently have an uphill battle in explaining their vision and methods. There are no widely understood terms referring to an egalitarian society without rulers.

The idea of "democracy" has had a similar but less drastic fate. For most people it has come to mean voting and elected representatives, which can be called electoral democracy or representative democracy. A form of democracy in which citizens have direct control over decisions has to have a different name, such as direct democracy or participatory democracy. There is an ongoing struggle over the meaning of "democracy." As social scientists say, its meaning is "essentially contested."

Because different groups have an interest in promoting certain ideas and certain meanings of ideas, it is not easy to promote socially beneficial simple ideas. There is an enormous intellectual challenge involved, but it is one that cannot take place solely among intellectuals. All sorts of people have to be involved in developing simple and useful ideas.

9

Celebrity intellectuals

It's better to think for oneself and to assess ideas on their own merits than to worry about whether they came from a famous intellectual or an unknown.

When I was much younger, I had illusions about people with good ideas. If I read a book that I thought expressed courageous and perceptive views, I generally assumed that the author was a "good" person—concerned, committed, and socially sensitive in various ways. As a result of numerous encounters over the years, I've had to toss out this belief.

A productive academic, "Freddo Carruthers," was a long-time champion of the ideas of Jürgen Habermas, who is noted for his support for the ideal of free speech. Carruthers on occasion wrote books and articles based on the ideas of his research students, without giving the students a chance to see his writing before it was published. Carruthers believed in the Ideal Speech Situation but, when it came to promoting his career, did not practise it with his students.

Another academic was widely known as an advocate of democratic communication. He was also known to female students as an incorrigible harasser. They called him a sleazebag and took care not to go into his office alone, since they might be pinned to the wall and groped.

Another communication scholar was widely known for his prolific contributions. Not so widely known was his love for young female students, who he used to bed down in his office through his declining years. He was also known to blackmail students, giving bad marks to those who refused his demands.

Paulo Freire was a well-known figure in the field of "critical pedagogy." He was widely respected and received substantial funding from various government organisations. Blanca Facundo, a supporter of critical pedagogy, wrote a critique of Freire's approach based on years of practical experience with the methods. This critique was well received by grassroots practitioners.[1] Freire responded with a personal attack on Facundo. Freire's followers ignored the critique and continued their largely uncritical support of the master.

Then there are the violent ones. One widely respected US left-wing figure often beat his partner. But when she spoke out about it, no one seemed to want to know. Louis Althusser, a famous French left-wing intellectual, killed his wife.[2]

All this is nothing new. Many renowned intellectuals and activists have had feet of clay. Karl Marx, champion of the working class, tried to maintain a bourgeois lifestyle by borrowing from friends. He was notorious for his authoritarian behaviour in personal relations and socialist politics.[3]

Michael Bakunin, one of the greatest figures in anarchism, was vehemently opposed to all governments. At the same time, he plotted incessantly, created all sorts of secret cells and had grandiose ideas of capturing power.[4]

The flaws and foibles of left-wing intellectuals have been catalogued at length by Max Nomad, who seems to have made a

---

[1] Blanca Facundo, *An Evaluation of Freire-Inspired Programs in the United States and Puerto Rico* (Puerto Rico: Latino Institute, 1984); http://www.uow.edu.au/arts/sts/bmartin/dissent/documents/Facundo/.

[2] Geraldine Finn, "Women and the ideology of science," *Our Generation,* Vol. 15, No. 1, Winter 1982, pp. 40-50.

[3] Jerrold Seigel, *Marx's Fate: The Shape of a Life* (Princeton: Princeton University Press, 1978).

[4] Alfred P. Mendel, *Michael Bakunin: Roots of Apocalypse* (New York: Praeger, 1981). This is only one interpretation of Bakunin's psychodynamics.

career out of puncturing illusions about those who see themselves as saviours of the workers.[5]

These examples are of male intellectuals, but females are not exempt. Marlene Dixon was a left-winger whose writings and activism were highly resented by male academics. In her book *Things Which Are Done in Secret* she wrote powerfully about the machinations used to get rid of her and others at McGill University.[6] Later she became head of a Marxist-Leninist organisation. It had lofty ideals of gender and ethnic equality as part of revolutionary struggle. Dissident party members, on the other hand, portrayed Dixon as an abusive autocrat and alcoholic, enjoying privileges not permitted to the rank and file.[7]

But does it matter? What difference does it make whether great ideas come from flawed humans?

One answer is that it makes little or no difference. The key thing is the ideas themselves, not who came up with them. It is certainly true that ideas often can be used without being contaminated by where they came from. In the same way, it is possible to enjoy Wagner's music or Picasso's paintings without being affected by the politics or sexual life of Wagner or Picasso.

Another answer is that it does matter. Knowing the origins of ideas can help in assessing the ideas themselves. For example, a close analysis of the social context of early Marxism provides clues to limitations in Marxist theory itself, especially the privileged role it gives to intellectuals.[8] A study of the social influences on Darwin's thought—Malthus's ideas of a competitive

---

5 Max Nomad, *Rebels and Renegades* (New York: Macmillan, 1932); Max Nomad, *Aspects of Revolt* (New York: Bookman Associates, 1959).

6 Marlene Dixon, *Things Which Are Done in Secret* (Montreal: Black Rose Books, 1976).

7 Peter Siegel, Nancy Strohl, Laura Ingram, David Roche and Jean Taylor, "Leninism as cult: the Democratic Workers Party," *Socialist Review,* Vol. 17, No. 6, November-December 1987, pp. 59-85.

8 Alvin W. Gouldner, *Against Fragmentation: The Origins of Marxism and the Sociology of Intellectuals* (New York: Oxford University Press, 1985).

struggle for survival were influential—provides insight into biases in evolutionary theory.[9]

To determine social influences on ideas can be a challenging task. There is no guarantee of finding anything in particular or anything at all. Even so, the behaviour of thinkers provides a basis for beginning an investigation. If communication scholars are plagiarists or sexual harassers, this does not automatically mean that communication theories are flawed. But if there are gross discrepancies between theory and behaviour, it is worthwhile finding out how they are justified or tolerated.

There is another way in which it matters that great ideas come from flawed individuals. It relates to the cult of celebrities.

Richard Schickel points out that the celebrity is a twentieth-century phenomenon, created especially by movies and television. He describes a culture of celebrity, in which people strive to be well known, even if this is only because they have appeared on the screen. The culture of celebrity, he argues, is undermining many traditional practices. For example, politicians are sold on the media in terms of image rather than policies.[10]

David Marshall argues that there is a system of celebrity which continues even though individuals come and go. The system depends on an interaction between celebrities and their audiences. The celebrity system is related to capitalism in that personality is made into a commodity.[11]

The cult of celebrities is making increasing inroads into scholarly circles. While many academics personally detest publicity about their work, some are gaining a public profile. At

9   Robert M. Young, "The historiographic and ideological contexts of the nineteenth-century debate on man's place in nature," in Mikuláš Teich and Robert M. Young (eds.), *Changing Perspectives in the History of Science: Essays in Honour or Joseph Needham* (London: Heinemann, 1973), pp. 344-438.

10 Richard Schickel, *Common Fame: The Culture of Celebrity* (London: Pavilion Books, 1985).

11 P. David Marshall, *Celebrity and Power: Fame in Contemporary Culture* (Minneapolis: University of Minnesota Press, 1997).

the highest level, a few become media stars, such as Carl Sagan and David Suzuki. Others become well known in particular circles. Nobel Prize winners become public figures. Suddenly their opinions become newsworthy, even when their views have little to do with their prize-winning research.

Rather than reading about ideas, it is increasingly common-place to read about the person who is associated with the ideas— a "personal profile." If an idea is not associated with a prominent thinker, it is more easily dismissed.

The cult of celebrity operates within academia itself. The latest intellectual fashions are typically associated with individuals, whether it is Jacques Derrida, Michel Foucault or Donna Haraway.

None of this is all that new. The striving for fame has been a tremendous driving force for centuries.[12] Technologies for mass communication, which gave rise to the modern celebrity, have been around for decades. Celebrity intellectuals are not new. They are just becoming more prevalent.

One consequence of this is that people are attracted to ideas because of the prominent intellectual who is associated with them. This is a mild version of what happens with various gurus and prophets. The followers have faith in their leader rather than thinking for themselves.

The other side of this dynamic is that if a person is shown to be flawed—a harasser, a plagiariser or just a snob—then this can serve to undermine the ideas they espouse. In other words, debates over ideas are pursued by attacking and defending the people associated with them.

Being a celebrity gives one a degree of power, and along with this comes various dangers. The first and most immediate risk for a famous person is to believe that one's fame is truly deserved on the basis of one's person rather than being due to the audience or historical circumstances. It is far easier to recognise

---

12 Leo Braudy, *The Frenzy of Renown: Fame and its History* (New York: Oxford University Press, 1986).

that some other successful person was simply the "right person in the right place at the right time" than it is to see one's own success in the same light.

Associated with this is a tendency towards arrogance and exclusivity. This can result in:

- not answering queries except from those who are prominent themselves (though, admittedly, some well-known figures are totally overwhelmed by requests);
- expecting special treatment in accommodation, travel and meetings;
- charging high fees when not needed financially;
- claiming credit for the work of assistants.

Another hazard is to encourage others to believe in one's ideas rather than to think for themselves. Most celebrities depend on many followers being uncritical, since otherwise they would not be followers. If people thought for themselves, they would be unlikely to depend so much on a few prominent figures for wisdom—and most celebrities would no longer be put on such a pedestal.

The next step is to attack others who disagree. This can be done by the celebrity or by followers. Sometimes this is an open attack. More commonly in intellectual circles, it takes the form of denying publication to those who are out of fashion. This is not a sin peculiar to celebrities. There are numerous cases in which scholars have taken the ideas of subordinates without acknowledgment, blocked appointments and spread rumours, all with the aim of getting ahead and squashing competitors.

A final problem for celebrities is that they can avoid responsibility for their failings. Usually this happens because friends and supporters, who are most likely to know about the failings, keep quiet because they do not want to fall out of favour or to give ammunition to critics.[13]

---

[13] These problems are also occupational hazards for gurus, who have similarities to celebrities. See Anthony Storr, *Feet of Clay: A Study of Gurus* (London: HarperCollins, 1996).

On the other hand, celebrities can be subject to unscrupulous attacks by jealous critics who hope to bring them down. Even trivial actions of celebrities can trigger exaggerated praise or criticism.

The power that celebrities wield is limited, because they are constantly at the mercy of those who make them into celebrities: editors, journalists and especially followers. Nevertheless, it is worthwhile doing what one can to limit celebrity power and its associated corruptions.

There are a few techniques that prominent intellectuals can use to defuse any cult of personality. One is to submit some of their writings under pseudonyms. Some famous authors—such as Doris Lessing—have tried this and found that their books are rejected when submitted under another name.

Much of the problem, though, is in the followers who look for salvation or illumination from individuals rather than common ideas and collective action. Much intellectual work examines the ideas of great thinkers rather than tracing the history of social processes.

Celebrity intellectuals gain power by being given credit for certain ideas. To challenge this power, one possible goal is to eliminate any power associated with credit for ideas. This sounds impossible in present-day society. Intellectuals publish articles and books and use this achievement to obtain degrees, appointments, promotions and research grants. To eliminate power from ideas, it would be necessary to move to an egalitarian society. In such a society, brilliant thinkers would still be listened to carefully, encouraged and recognised, but they would have no extra formal power as a result of their contributions to intellectual life. They might have fame but no associated power.

An alternative goal, perhaps more achievable, is to encourage everyone to think for themselves.[14] This goal is often stated by

---

[14] *The Revolutionary Pleasure of Thinking for Yourself* (Tucson, AZ: See Sharp Press, 1992).

educational administrators, but in practice students are more commonly encouraged to think like their teachers. Those who question standard ideas are usually discouraged.

There are several things an individual can do to break the habit of idolising a few thinkers.

- Get a friend to give you material with the author's name removed. Focus on the ideas without worrying about who thought them up and expressed them.

- Look for the weaknesses and omissions in the most popular ideas. Look for useful aspects of unfashionable and rejected ideas.

- If the author is famous, be especially critical. If the author is unknown or stigmatised, be especially open to useful contributions. Try to counteract the tendency to judge ideas by their origins, while still taking account of the influence of origins.

- Make a special effort to give credit to "unknowns" who have similar (or better) ideas than celebrity intellectuals.

- Remember that social change comes from the actions of many people, not just ideas from a few individuals.

10

Toward information liberation

Information seems like the ideal basis for a cooperative society. It can be made available to everyone at low cost, and a person can give away information and still retain use of it. In practice, information is an important part of struggles over power, wealth and authority. Some people are able to speak through the mass media while most others are only listeners. Bureaucrats control information in order to control subordinates and clients. Surveillance is a process of collecting information in order to exert power.

In order to bring about a more just and equal society, struggles need to be waged over information. It would be nice to call the goal "freedom of information." Unfortunately, that phrase is already taken over by legislation that is supposed to allow citizens access to government documents. FOI legislation has not been very successful in opening up government to public scrutiny. Politicians and government bureaucrats have restricted access in various ways, including charging fees that make a mockery of the name "freedom of information." Even if FOI worked perfectly, it is a very limited freedom, since it does nothing about corporate secrecy, defamation law, surveillance and ownership of information.

Since the expression "freedom of information" has been degraded, perhaps it is better to talk of "information liberation," which is the general project of using information to move toward a society free of domination. It doesn't make much sense to say that information itself is oppressed. Rather, information is often a means of domination of both humans and the environment. The goal is to make information into a tool for liberation.

Information liberation should be thought of as a process rather than an end point. What helps today in one place to move towards a better society might not be appropriate later or somewhere else. However, even though there's no universal strategy, it can be helpful to look at some lessons from the previous chapters. I present these ideas as tentative proposals, for discussion and debate.

Live the alternative

One powerful way to move towards an alternative is to begin behaving as if it already exists. If the goal is a society based on interactive network media, then it is helpful to support and use those media. If the goal is a society in which there is no censorship to serve vested interests, then it is helpful to support free speech and not to resort to censorship or defamation proceedings oneself.

It is always easy to criticise someone else's attacks on one's own speech. It is much harder to recognise the corruptions of power when one has the power oneself.

Work on the inside and outside

Setting up alternative media is valuable but it's also necessary to operate within mainstream media to bring about change. To change bureaucratic controls over information, an alliance of employees and outside activists is quite powerful. There is no single best location for action for every person. Some people are independent of institutions and free to make strong statements or take public actions. Others are inside powerful organisations and can best bring about change by working carefully behind the scenes.

There are traps for both insiders and outsiders. The big danger for insiders is becoming part of the system and serving to prop it up. How many managers in publishing or biotechnology firms seek anything other than maximum intellectual property rights? How many police or marketeers seek to restrain surveillance? On the other hand, if insiders go too far in questioning the system, they may lose their influence and perhaps their careers. Challenging things from the inside is a delicate business.

From the outside, it's possible to be much more outspoken. But there is a risk in becoming negative and self-righteous—in speaking out in order to feel good but without being effective in bringing about change.

Be participatory

If the aim is open organisations, free speech, interactive media and useful ideas, then it's important to involve as many people as possible in the process of bringing them about. It's not wise to rely on experts to do the job. Experts on defamation law reform or on avoiding surveillance can be very helpful, but can't bring about change on their own. If speech is to be freed from defamation threats, surveillance and bureaucratic controls, plenty of people must exercise their speech in the process of bringing about the change.

Naturally, there's always a role for the individual activist, such as the whistleblower who speaks out when others are afraid. But the lesson from the experience of whistleblowers is that most of them are severely penalised and lead to no change in the problem. A collective challenge is far more powerful. Building a campaign that can involve lots of people is the only way that major systems of information power, such as mass media and intellectual property, will ever be transformed.

Change both individuals and social structures

Individual change is vital to social change. So part of the process is engaging with friends, neighbours, colleagues, clients and others in order to raise ideas and try out behaviours. Support groups and campaigns can be effective in bringing about individual change. A campaign to challenge defamation law or promote community-oriented research is a tremendous way to learn about the issues, sort out ideas and learn how the system works.

Included in individual change is one's own self. It is one thing to bring about change in others and another to bring about change in one's own beliefs and behaviours.

Individual change is important, but so is change in social structures, which includes families, governments, capitalism, racism and patriarchy, among others. Within these big and pervasive social structures, significant changes are possible, such as in laws, bureaucratic mandates and products. Social structures are not fixed. Instead, they are just ways of talking about regularities in actions and ideas. They can be changed, but it's not easy.

Individuals affect the dynamics of social structures, which in turn affect the way individuals operate. So it's important to have a process of changing both.

These four suggested ideas for bringing about information liberation are not the final word. There are always exceptions, such as occasions to use the mass media or rely on experts. Furthermore, there are frictions between the ideas. Working for change on the inside of a large media organisation is valuable, but it is not exactly living the alternative. That's to be expected. Total self-consistency would leave little room for creative approaches.

My final recommendation is to have fun along the way. Trying to bring about a better world can be depressing, with constant reminders about the massive amount of corruption, injustice and violence that exists. Yet part of the goal of a better society is one in which there is more joy and laughter. Living the alternative means having fun along the way, whether that means exposing the absurdities of defamation law or bureaucracies or designing humorous stunts. There are certainly plenty of opportunities in the process of information liberation.

Index

UPROOTING WAR

by Brian Martin

UPROOTING WAR is unlike the numerous treatments of the dangers of war, the benefits of disarmament or the need for government or citizen action. It is about developing strategies for grassroots activists to challenge and replace the war system. Brian Martin presents a wide-ranging critical analysis of social institutions and, as well, draws upon his experiences as a social activist.

The peace movement has used methods such as lobbying, rallies and civil disobedience. All of this has been important, but it has had little impact on military races. The trouble is that only a few campaigns seriously challenge the hierachical power structures which underlie preparations and resort to war.

UPROOTING WAR aims to encourage serious thinking about strategies against war which involve confronting institutions such as the state, bureaucracy, the military and patriarchy. Some of the alternative directions examined are social defence, peace conversion, and building self-managing political and economic institutions.

The author also presents some controversial proposals for politically preparing for the actuality of nuclear war while at the same time helping to reduce its likelihood.

298 pages **FREEDOM PRESS** ISBN 0 900384 26 3 £5.00

STRIP THE EXPERTS

by Brian Martin

During the past couple of decades 'professional services' have been the fastest growing sector of employment. You can't do much in modern Western societies without coming into contact with (it's usually against) experts.

Brian Martin writes from his experience as an expert and in handling other experts. His illustrations are drawn from personal experience. In essence he is encouraging us to think and act for ourselves in the face of professional opposition. He encourages the reader to challenge the expert's facts, use counter examples and point to uncertainties. He recommends identifying the expert's assumptions and questioning them. He wants us to put the expert under the magnifying glass in pointing to his inconsistencies, vested interests and the irrelevance of his expertise to the question in hand. He advises us to find out about our expert opposition because the search will often reveal how incompetent and stupid he is and give us more confidence in fighting our own corner.

69 pages **FREEDOM PRESS** ISBN 0 900384 63 8 £1.95

SOCIAL *DEFENCE*
SOCIAL CHANGE

by Brian Martin

The idea of social defence – namely of abolishing military forces and relying in their stead on non-violent struggles by the general population – is extemely radical. Yet seldom before have the many radical implications of social defence been outlined.

Social Defence, Social Change argues for social defence as a grassroots initiative linked to challenges to oppressive structures in society such as patriachy, police and the state. Filled with examples from Finland to Fiji, the book also provides a provocative survey of radical alternatives in politics and economics.

Social defence is not just a defence option. It is a direction for action that should be known to all those who seek a society without oppression, inequality or violence.

157 pages **FREEDOM PRESS** ISBN 0 900384 69 7 £4.95